HOMESICK

HOMESICK

A MEMOIR

SELA WARD

ReganBooks
An Imprint of HarperCollinsPublishers

Grateful acknowledgment is made for permission to reprint the following copyrighted material: lyrics from "Avalon Blues" by Mississippi John Hurt, © and renewed by Wynwood Music Co., Inc. Used by permission.

All photos courtesy of the Ward family, with the following exceptions (all used by permission): pp. iii, 184, 186 © Beth D. Carr; pp. 4, 159, 163, 258 © Melanie Acevedo; p. 107 courtesy Wilhelmina/Hank Londoner/Rotem; p. 118 © Rob Cohen; p. 135 courtesy CBS Photo Archive; p. 144 © 1992 Jack Caputo Photography; p. 173 © Paula Merritt/*Meridian Star*; pp. 176–7, 182 courtesy of the City of Meridian, Office of the Mayor; p. 251 © Orit Harpaz. *Color insert:* p. 6 © Paul Carrino; p. 7 © Jacques Silberstein; p. 9 © Jack Caputo Photography; p. 10 (top) © 1996 Warner Bros., All Rights Reserved, (bottom left) © Frank Trapper/Corbis Sygma, (bottom right) © Craig T. Mathew/ATAS; p. 11 © Touchstone Television; p. 14 © Melanie Acevedo; p. 15 © Peter Kredenser; p. 16 © Melanie Acevedo.

HarperCollins books may be purchased for educational, business, or sales promotional use. For information please write: Special Markets Department, HarperCollins Publishers Inc., 10 East 53rd Street, New York, NY 10022.

FIRST EDITION

Designed by Christine Sullivan

Printed on acid-free paper

Library of Congress Cataloging-in-Publication Data has been applied for.

ISBN 0-06-039436-6

02 03 04 05 06 WBC/RRD 10 9 8 7 6 5 4 3 2 1

To my siblings, Jenna, Berry, and Brock; my daddy, G. H.; and most of all to my mama—who showed me in heart, mind, and soul what a home truly was . . .

And to my children, Austin and Anabella, and to my husband, Howard, who show me every day and in every way what a home truly is . . .

Acknowledgments

If they say it takes a village to raise a child, it truly takes a city, state, or nation to birth a book. And while I spent so much time at the computer that I finally became familiar with the inner and outer workings of Word, without the assistance, support, and encouragement of my team, this book would have remained just a dream.

I pay tribute to the people who helped me to urge this story into the light of day and onto paper. I thank you and I love you, for I would not be writing these acknowledgments without you. . . .

Rod Dreher—my friend, who helped give structure and voice to the story I wanted to tell, and whose own Southern roots enriched the who, what, where, when, and how of the final product.

Cal Morgan—my amazing editor, who guided me back onto the

path when I strayed, and who helped me in countless ways to tell the broader story through the details of my life experiences.

Joni Evans—my fabulous agent, who fought for and won me the freedom and time to tell the story that I wanted to tell.

Judith Regan—my ever-talented publisher, who started it all with an offer and followed it up with belief and support in the book that I really wanted to write.

David Seltzer—my manager, who read and critiqued the book so many times he practically has it committed to memory.

Aunt Nancy and Uncle Joe—who shared their love, their stories, and their insight into our family.

Hallie Ward—my sister-in-law, for spinning her tales, and for the love and laughter she adds to the family.

Kate and Val—raconteurs extraordinaire, who brought life and a third dimension to the colorful and eccentric side of being Southern, and who kept me hysterically laughing through much of the research portion of the book.

Jackie Moses—my assistant, whose many mad dashes to FedEx and late-night sessions combing through boxes and boxes of photos saved the day time after time.

Manny and Melanie Mitchell—for reminding me that you don't catch brim with minnows, and a number of other good ol' Southern notes.

Rina Freedman—for the gift of amazing wisdom and contribution to my life and thus to this book.

Patrick Sinclair—who rode in like the cavalry at the eleventh hour to lend his unique insight and perspective and sense of humor just before the book wrapped.

Carrie Wiatt—a two-time author who shared her experiences in the writing process and the perseverance required.

And finally, to my husband, Howard, who encouraged me when I was tired, who helped me when I was weary, and who found just the right turn of phrase when I was stuck.

I love y'all....
Sela

HOMESICK

P art of me never left
and another part is always leaving,
leaving Mississippi but never gone.
"Jimmy when you gonna come on back
down home," my people ask,
and I cannot say, "Never,
I've found my home somewhere else"
Anymore than I can say home
Was never in the State of Mississippi
But in the community of it . . .

—James Autry,
"Leaving Mississippi"

With Jenna, Berry, and Brock.

This is a story about home.

It is the story of a girl raised in a gentle town in the Deep South, cradled by family and friends, worshiping Bear Bryant on Saturday night and Jesus Christ on Sunday morning, savoring sweet tea and porch swings, corn bread and courtesy and all the tender mercies of a Mississippi childhood.

That girl grew up and moved to the big city. Her destiny took her north to New York, and then west to southern California. She became a well-known actress, married a long, tall, handsome beau, and started a family.

And midway through her life's journey, this girl who thought she had everything—me—began to realize what she'd been missing. Which is to say, the good, indeed irreplaceable, things I had left behind in the South.

Truth to tell, it wasn't that I lacked these things; they have been in my heart and soul all my life. But in the busy-ness of my Hollywood life, I had forgotten them. And one day, it snuck up on me that I was well and truly homesick.

I don't think I'm alone in this. So many of us have moved away from the modest place that was too small to hold our dreams, too quiet for the noise we were born to make. Yet for all the success we may have found in the big city (or sprawling suburb), we are discovering there is a cost.

We have strayed too far from the humble things that endure, and given short shrift to the rituals and traditions that give meaning and continuity to our lives.

These are things that you can't buy at Pottery Barn, or manufacture with the advice of Martha Stewart. They are virtues forged in the hearth of a loving home, and which must be renewed from father to son, from mother to daughter, from age to age. Whether we have moved down the street or across the country from our birthplace, we have strayed too far from home.

And it's time to turn back.

I'm not talking about moving back to our hometowns. For some people that can be an appealing option, but it's one that is closed to many of us, and for most of us it wouldn't necessarily be the right thing to do—after all, there was a reason we left in the first place. What I'm talking about is re-creating, wherever we now live, the best parts of home, either the home we had growing up, or the home we wished for. Home as a place of shelter and comfort, both physically and spiritually. Home as a well from which a family draws its emotional strength to face the challenges of the day and the hardships of a lifetime.

I want to tell you about my home—or homes, really, because as much as I love the South, there's no denying that part of me is also at home in southern California, where I work and live with my husband and children most of the year. Still, though I'm not *in* the South most of the time, I am undeniably *of* the South. Its customs and ways have shaped me as sure as the great Mississippi formed the Delta. And it is to the South I always return when I need comfort, solace, and respite from the rigors of city life.

When I'm feeling burned out, thrown out of balance by life in Los Angeles, I think of the line from the old gospel song, sung throughout the South since forever: "Come home, come home, ye who are weary come home." Well, I am weary, and I miss home. Here, then, is the story of a prodigal daughter who finally understood how much she loved her Southern home and needed it, to make sense of her life in parts unknown. "Home is where one starts from," said T. S. Eliot. And, I am finding, where one ends up.

The train rocks gently as I write this, its rails carrying me back from Los Angeles to New Orleans to visit old friends and family. I find no comfort in flying these days. Instead I'm grateful for these forty hours of calm. In my mind, for just a moment, I'm back on the old Southerner line of my childhood days, taking that joyous forty-

five-minute adventure from Meridian to Laurel, Mississippi, safe in knowing that my parents would be there to meet me when I arrived. I close my eyes and remember the crisp white tablecloths of the elegant dining car, the napkins and silver and small vase of flowers. Then I open them and through the window glimpse a small-town street in southeastern Arizona—pickup trucks and bucking-bronco café signs, a schoolkid running across the street, backpack in tow, beneath the green shade of a sycamore.

When we get to New Orleans, I will meet my sister, then begin the drive north to Meridian, my hometown. So many times I've made this trip since Mama's health took a turn for the worse, but never have I needed it more than now. My heart is tender these days; I yearn for a string of lazy afternoons on the front porch of our farm cottage, a glass of sweet tea in my hand, with nothing to do but watch the dragonflies light on the nickel-silver surface of the pond, loll in the humid, earthy air, and let it draw the sweat to the surface of my skin. I need to hear the sound of a late-summer rain on a tin roof, and the sweet chorus of crickets and bullfrogs at sunset.

I need to draw closer. I need to be back among my family—to gather the older generations with the younger, all around the same hearth. I need to listen to funny stories about crazy old aunts, to hear the soft cadences of Southern voices, to taste my native-born accent in my mouth again, and to have the waitress at the Waffle House ask me if I want grits with that, honey.

Because I need all these things as I need the air that I breathe, I'm headed south once again. South, toward home.

The place where I am and the place I know, and other places that familiarity with and love for my own make strange and lovely and enlightening to look into, are what set me to writing my stories.

—Eudora Welty

Hunting for Easter eggs.

1 ❧

....

Ask any Southern woman to tell you about herself, and she'll start by telling you about her people. The roots of my family tree run deep into the red dirt of Mississippi, and from the time I was born to the moment I left home for college, I was surrounded and sheltered by its branches: parents and grandparents, aunts and uncles, Boswells and Wards. As a child I listened keenly to their stories, though I was shy and quiet and asked questions only rarely. Now, with so few of them left, I spend as much time in their company as I can, and I ask everything I can think of.

There have been Wards living in and around Meridian for six generations—since the 1840s, as best as my daddy can figure. His great-grandfather was the first Ward to live in this part of Mississippi;

the wooden homestead he built still stands on its cypress-log pillars in the tiny community called Enterprise, eighteen miles south of Meridian on Ward Road. My daddy's generation calls it Homeward.

The house is small by today's standards, but once it was part of a six-hundred-acre plantation that extended to the banks of the Chunky River. Today the family holdings are a fragment of what they were, but Homeward is still there, home to Daddy's sister Celeste and her husband, Fred. In the yard there are fig trees and magnolias, and lilies that Aunt Celeste tends like children. At the edge of the property stands a cypress barn that's been there longer than my seventy-nine-year-old father can remember. At one time the field was filled with cotton and cornstalks, but it's been many years since this was a working farm.

Though he lived in Meridian as a boy, my daddy, Granberry Holland Ward Jr., loves this land as if it had always been his. In a sense, it has. All his relatives lived in Enterprise. "I would go out to Grandpa's house every time I'd go down there," he remembers. "He was a justice of the peace for fifty years. They called him Judge Ward. He married just about all the couples in Clark County. They would come out to his house to get married. He had a wagon that was pulled by mules. He lived about three miles out of town, and when he needed to go into town he would let me drive, holding the reins all the way."

When he was a teenager Daddy would ride his bicycle to Enterprise, up and down fifteen miles of hills, to see his cousin James; the two of them were best friends. "We'd go skinny-dipping in a little creek that goes through the town there. It had a kind of deep part in it, and we would dive off in the water, swim there."

James was a popular boy in Enterprise. "He dated every little girl there, before he went in the service." But he got into a little mischief now and then. "He told me the girls would sit at a certain spot at the school, and when they'd have a short dress on, you could see up their leg, you know?" Did Daddy succumb to the same temptation? "I didn't ever know where that spot was," he laughs. "I never did sit there. I was a good boy."

Then, when Daddy was seven years old, came a day whose every detail he still remembers. He and his sister were outside at half-past four in the afternoon, laughing and dousing each other with a garden hose, when their mother came out to tell them their father had just died. It wasn't a sudden death; he had suffered from encephalitis for months. But the news transformed Daddy's life. For years thereafter, he recalls, "Wherever I was out playing, at 4:30 in the afternoon I'd run home and see if Mama was still living."

The concept of orphanhood was familiar to Daddy's family: his own first name, Granberry, came from the man who ran the orphanage where his grandmother—Judge Ward's wife—was raised. After his own father died, Daddy says, "The lady across the street told my mother, 'It's too bad your husband died—I know you're going to have to put all your children in the orphans' home.' That kept her all upset all the time." That never happened, but their father's death changed the family all the same: Daddy's seventeen-year-old brother, Thomas, had to go out and find work to support them all, taking a job at a lumber mill during the day and at a drugstore until ten o'clock at night. It was Daddy's job to bring his older brother his lunch every day; during the summer he hopped from lawn to lawn to save his bare feet from the sun-cooked sidewalks.

I remember, throughout my own childhood, listening quietly as Daddy and his kin told and retold stories about those times. It was the Depression, but "we didn't know we were poor," Daddy says. "We didn't know we didn't have anything, and for some reason it didn't matter. People were closer because we were all suffering in the same boat. I don't remember anybody feeling like they were better than the family next door. We had a big two-story house, and plenty of room to take others in. We took several children and their mother into our home when I was young, because of adverse conditions. It was no big thing."

Daddy's Aunt Margaret, his cousin James's mother, was like a second mother to him. When I was a child Daddy and Mama would take us down to Enterprise visiting Homeward on Sunday afternoons, and at least once a month we'd stop by Aunt Margaret's on the way back. I was so fascinated with her rambling yellow Victorian clapboard house. It always seemed dark to me; she never really had the lights on, and being there was like stepping back in time. The rooms were full of dark old furniture, embroidered settees, and stacks of handmade quilts everywhere; whenever I visited I'd find an excuse to go into the bathroom, just to stare at the porcelain pitchers and old-fashioned washbasins from the days before houses had running water.

What everybody remembers about Aunt Margaret, though, was her passion for canning. Her kitchen shelves were lined with all types of fruits and vegetables—relishes and jams, tomatoes and figs and sweet pear relish. "If you ever went to her house," Daddy remembers, "you would always leave with something in your hand. She would give you some gift of food. She just loved people." The same was true in my childhood, thirty years later. The figs and relishes I accepted politely, but I couldn't wait to get hold of her black-berry jam.

Daddy may have been a carefree country boy, but he was fasci-nated with electricity. He started teaching himself the basics of electrical engineering when he was twelve. By the time World War II came around he'd begun working at AT&T, where he was given a deferment from military service in light of the value of his services on the home front. But that all soon changed. In 1943 cousin James stopped by Daddy's house to announce that he was going into the navy. And as he he walked away, he turned back and told Daddy he felt sure he wasn't coming back. Ten months later, he was training on a torpedo bomber off the coast of California when he was killed in an accident. My father's voice still quavers with the emotion of that day. The loss was devastating to Aunt Margaret. "Every time she'd see me right after that, she'd start crying," Daddy says, "'cause we had played together all our lives." Not long thereafter, Daddy enlisted. "I went in because he got killed," Daddy says. "I just couldn't stay out after that."

He spent a year and a half in the Navy, training with the Amphibious Corps in the South Pacific. As the best radar operator on his ship—and the only one capable of both using radar and maintain-ing the equipment—Daddy got kid-glove treatment. "When it came time to go into port and scrub the bottom of the boat and repaint it," he chuckles, "I'd go climb in my bunk and take a nap. They wouldn't bother me—they wanted me to be fresh for anything they needed on the conning tower. So I would get out of all that work."

Daddy in the navy.

Daddy always marched to his own drummer, as his fellow crew-
men were finding out. "We were donated a lot of records from a high
school in New Jersey," he remembers. "We took turns playing music
for the whole ship. I would play classical music, although nobody else
liked it but me and a few others. So when they heard Tchaikovsky or
Chopin blaring from the speakers, they always knew who was in the
conning tower." The conditions of wartime sea travel also earned
Daddy a nickname. "We didn't have enough water on board; we had
to make our own, out of salt water. And we couldn't shave for long
lengths of time. So everybody grew a beard. But at that age all I could
grow was a goatee. And me being from the South, the guys nick-
named me The Colonel. On the PA system you'd hear, '*Colonel Ward,
forward to the conning tower . . .* ' The captain of the ship was only a lieu-
tenant junior grade, so everyone really got a kick out of it."

Colonel Ward and the rest of his troop of sailors were training for
an invasion of the home islands of Japan. But when the atomic bomb
was dropped in 1945 and Japan surrendered, the invasion was scotched.
When Daddy returned home he applied to the Massachusetts Insti-
tute of Technology, but postwar competition was fierce among the
returning vets, and a single B on his transcript was enough to keep
him out of MIT. Daddy went to Georgia Tech instead, earned his
degree in electrical engineering, and came back home to Meridian.

In 1953, G.H. (as everybody calls him) met a dark-haired beauty
named Annie Kate Boswell. She would become his wife, and not
long thereafter my mother. And the story of Mama's background
affected me at least as profoundly as my father's.

Mama's brother Joe, six years younger than she, is an avid story-teller in the Southern mold, and many of his best yarns go back to the earliest years of the Depression—a time that hit the Boswells harder than the Wards. Their family moved all over Meridian in those years, going from house to house, trying to find a comfortable berth in a time when it must have seemed nearly impossible to keep a family afloat. "Every time the rent come due, we'd move, you know . . ." he laughs now. And their life was made doubly difficult by an accident that occurred when Joe was three.

"You know, everything back then was dirt roads, gravel. There were still teams of horses on the roads, you know, and the Coca-Cola Company used to pull all these cartons from Meridian all the way over to Alabama, forty miles away, by horse team. My mother was a *good* driver; she would drive that route all the time. But Daddy was driving that day.

"Now, this old guy that drove for Coca-Cola was driving a team of horses up ahead. And as Daddy passed him it stirred up so much dust, Daddy ran off the road into the ditch. Knocked Mother's hip out of place. Today you'd just go to the hospital and they'd reset a hip like that, you know. But back then they couldn't do anything like that. So for the rest of Mama's life her one leg was shorter than the other one, and she walked on crutches."

The trauma of the incident rocked my mama's family, but what Uncle Joe remembers is the Southern stoicism of his mother—and the kindness of that old driver. "He used to come by the house and ask about Miss Annie," he recalls. "He was crazy about Mama. He was so sorry that it happened. For years and years, he'd come and see Mama—you know, see how she was."

That was my mama's mama: Annie Raye Boswell. By all accounts she was an extraordinary woman, whose physical limitations seem never to have cost her an ounce of determination. "Bless her heart," Joe says with wonder. "Raised all five of us kids during the Depression and everything, crippled like that—and never complained. Walked to work, all the way to town and back on those crutches, every day. That's the kind of woman she was. Beautiful woman."

And her husband, Joe and Annie Kate's father, seems to have given her a run for her money for sheer tenaciousness. A sometime carpenter, sometime painter, he never met a job he wouldn't take. "Daddy was a little old bitty guy," Joe says. "Didn't weigh but ninety-one pounds when he was twenty-one years old. But he had arms 'bout twice as big as mine, 'cause he's hammering all the time. And he could build any-thing. He'd build a house from scratch—start at the bottom and go clear on up. Real confident, you know. They'd say, 'Mr. Boswell, can you do this?' 'Why, hell *yeah*, I can do it. What do you mean *can I do it?*' He never said he couldn't do anything. Tough as a nickel steak."

It was the early 1930s, and like many families the Boswells couldn't afford their own car. "Didn't have a truck, nothing. Daddy walked all over the town. He walked from this end of town to that end with a ladder on one shoulder, and a tool bag over the other. I'd be on the job with him in the summer, when I wasn't in school. He'd be wearing a little worker's hat, and sometimes we'd have to catch a bus to go 'cross town. He'd have that ladder on his shoulder, right there on the bus. And you know how you get embarrassed easy when you're that age. 'This your daddy?' people'd ask. And I'd say, 'No.'"

It wasn't easy for the Boswells to keep their children in food and clothing during those lean years—never mind taking care of them at

My mother, Annie Kate Boswell.

holiday time. One year, Joe remembers, his parents got him a wonderful Christmas gift: a new pair of roller skates, the old-fashioned,
adjustable kind that strapped on to your shoes. He held them in his
hands, marveling at how bright and shiny they seemed compared to
his old pair. The following year he got a second wonderful gift:
another new pair of skates. And then he realized what had happened. Each year, without his knowing it, his mother and father had
taken his old skates, cleaned them, oiled them, and put them back
under the tree. They could have told the kids that there was no
money for anything, and let it go at that. But it would have broken
their hearts not to be able to leave each of their children something
special under the tree—and so they found a way to do it.

Everybody who knew Miss Annie, as my grandmother was
called, saw the reflection of her strong and selfless spirit in my
mother, Annie Kate. "She and Annie Kate are so much alike it's
unreal, you know," Joe remembers. "It was never *What can you do
for me?* It was *What can I do for you?* I mean, they were just beautiful
people, both of them." Before she was out of high school, Annie
Kate was already working in Kress's, the local department store.
And she was also helping her mother keep a sharp eye on her brothers. "All four of us boys coming up, you know—you didn't go out of
the house till Annie Kate approved of you. Didn't date too much
back then, because we didn't have no way to go 'less it's by the city
bus. But you go out of that house, you got to look right, you know."

G. H. Ward and Annie Kate Boswell made quite a handsome
couple. Daddy was tall and thin, with a courtly demeanor, a strong

jaw that conveyed confidence, and an intelligence that illuminated his blue eyes. Mama was petite, with olive skin, raven-black hair, vivacious eyes, and a beautiful smile she framed all her life with her signature lipstick color, Revlon Love That Red. Mama was shy in public, but privately she had a feisty sense of humor, which surely bewitched my dad when they were dating. She, in turn, must have been drawn to his solidity. They saw each other for a year before they married on May 8, 1954, and settled down to start a family.

Soon Mama was pregnant, and in 1955 she gave birth prematurely to a son they named David. He lived for twenty-seven hours. Had that little boy been born today, he likely would have survived. But this was the mid-1950s, and a small-town Mississippi hospital wasn't equipped to give premature babies adequate care. Doctors told Mama and Daddy to try to have another baby as soon as possible, to help her get over the loss. They did, and I came into the world on July 11, 1956.

"I was so relieved when you were born," Daddy told me once. "I was so afraid you were going to die. I would go look in the baby bed all the time to see if you were still breathing."

Three more children—first Jenna, then Granberry III ("Berry"), and Brock—followed quickly, and Mama found herself with four kids, all under the age of six. I once asked Daddy if he ever considered relocating, moving away to raise his children elsewhere. "Never," he laughed. "This is home." It really was as simple as that for Daddy, and for so many Southerners of generations past. It was easier for him to imagine not existing at all than to imagine existing outside his beloved Mississippi home. But when it came to day-to-day family obligations, of course, most of the decisions fell to my

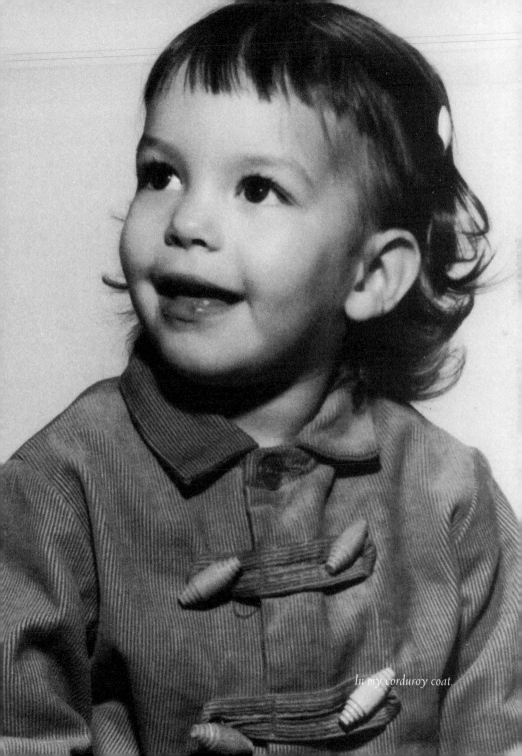

In my corduroy coat.

mother. "Your mama did all the raising of you kids," Daddy admits today. "The father was the one who brought the money home."

While Mama raised us children, Daddy labored in his engineer's office. The boom in postwar construction made Meridian fertile ground for an electrical engineer, and by the mid-1950s he had his hands full of work. But it wasn't an easy business to manage; as a subcontractor, he often didn't get paid till months after a job was completed. "I had to go to the bank and establish a line of credit" when he started, he told me not long ago. "And as I finished a job, I would go and pledge a fee to the bank, and go on to another job. I did that for years—that's how I raised y'all. It seemed like every Monday morning I was overdrawn." It wasn't until the 1970s, when he got into a different business—cable television—that all that changed.

Daddy was an ambitious man, and proud of his vocation; by the 1960s he had one of the top engineering firms in the state. But his work was extremely stressful, and many of his fellow engineers died young. A lot of them, Daddy included, drank too much to cope with the anxiety. A dear friend of his, a man Daddy says was the best engineer he ever knew, died in his early forties from an ulcerated stomach. I don't think Daddy has ever gotten over it.

Daddy's office was just a short walk through the woods from our house. I loved going to visit him there, loved the flat chemical smell of his blueprint ink. Even today I can remember standing on the log bridge that crossed the little creek behind the office, staring up at the sight of my father framed by a glass picture window, working away at his drafting board. He had a small printed sign on the wall that said BE REASONABLE: DO IT MY WAY. The Wards have always walked a fine line between conviction and orneriness, and Daddy was no exception.

Daddy was naturally a loner, even a bit of an eccentric, and his difficult ways could get him into trouble. He loved his bourbon at cocktail time, but alcohol wasn't a friend to Daddy. It made him contrary and angry. If relatives were over to visit, without blinking an eye he'd get up without excusing himself and go to bed, regardless of how anyone else—like my mother—felt about it. And things weren't necessarily all that much easier if he stayed: he had a tough analytical mind, and if he got it into his head to prove a point, he had a way of pressing and pressing you on it, often to the point of discomfort. He's always seemed so naturally wintry and introspective that I've often thought he would have been better off as a flinty New Englander.

But Daddy's cranky idiosyncrasies could veer off into more entertaining directions, too. He's always been obsessed with the weather. If snow was forecast as far away as Tennessee, he'd bundle the whole family into the car and take off for the border, six hours away. When we arrived he'd stop the car, get out in the snow, let it fall in his face, take a good long look, climb back in, then turn around and head home. Autumn is his favorite season; when I moved to New York in my twenties, Daddy would come visit me in the fall and drive out to Connecticut to see the brilliant foliage, which never appears in the South in quite the same way.

It does get cold down there, though, and when the thermometer

With Daddy.

dipped low enough for the first time each fall, Daddy couldn't wait to
build a roaring fire in our fireplace. The whole family would gather
around, and we'd talk, or not talk, and be together there around the
hearth. It was a ritual for the Wards. To this day I'm unable to take
pleasure in a gas fireplace; I was spoiled early by the crackle and pop
of real logs, the smell of burning oak and pine I still remember so well.

Even more than the fireplace, there was one place where Daddy
and I really connected, and that was his porch swing. He had a big
Mississippi State weather thermometer on the porch, and used to sit
in the swing and talk to me about . . . well, the weather. I'd lean into
him, and he would point to clouds in the sky, and tell me how they
were formed, and what kind of weather was on the way. It was there,

sitting on the swing with Daddy, that I first realized that he was envisioning a future for me, even before I did. He used to brainstorm business ideas for me. When he realized I had artistic inclinations, I remember him suggesting I might start my own architectural rendering firm. All he wanted was to make sure I'd end up my own boss, just as he had.

Daddy was also the first one to sense that I might need work on my self-confidence. During my teenage years, he encouraged me to work on my voice. "You sound so timid," he'd tell me. "When you pick up the phone and say 'Hi, this is Sela,' you sound like you're apologizing." To help strengthen my voice, he encouraged me to read aloud as often as possible. "When I was young, one of the jobs I had was to proofread written specifications," he recalls now. "So I had to read aloud an hour at a time. It gets you where you can talk easily. So I thought it'd be a good thing for you children to do the same."

What Daddy really taught us, though, was to have the courage of our convictions. In 1947, during a semester at Mississippi State, he was invited to pledge a fraternity. But when he found out that they weren't going to let a friend in because he was Jewish, he refused to join. "I just liked the fella," he says. "I couldn't believe they were treating him that way, and I didn't want any part of it." He didn't make a big to-do over it; he just walked away.

Daddy, then, was the strong and silent type, as they said in the movies. Mama was strong, too, but there was nothing silent about her.

Despite the difficult circumstances of her youth, Mama had an indomitable sense of pride, a regal bearing and steely dignity that made an enormous impression on me. She was incredibly beautiful: she looked in her youth like Ava Gardner, and pictures from her teenage years, when her family was still struggling, show her in stunning dresses hand-sewn for her by her mother. But what was most impressive about Annie Kate was that iron will of hers. Even into her old age, through nine years of sickness, nothing dimmed the fierce light in Mama's eyes.

There's an old saying in the South: "Remember who you are." Contained in those four words is an entire way of life that most Southerners feel in their bones. It says that whatever the external facts of your life, your soul can remain untouchable, your character intact, if you refuse to yield to despair and vulgarity. Mama had firm beliefs about the way the world worked, and strict expectations for her children. Virtue, kindliness, and self-discipline were paramount for her.

From the earliest age, Mama made sure we knew how we were expected to behave. As a schoolgirl, I remember sharing a carpool with other little girls from the neighborhood. One of the girls— whose family, Mama would point out, did not come from the South—got angry one day and called the mom who was driving a shockingly nasty name.

"Sela, you can't play with that girl anymore," Mama told me. With tears running down my cheeks, I pleaded with her to reconsider. But Mama's decision was final, as it always was. She said she knew this was tough on me, but that sort of behavior was intolerable, and she saw to it that her family distanced itself from children who disrespected adults and themselves so much.

Today that may seem like an overreaction to some. But Mama was about nothing if she wasn't about right and wrong, and she had an uncanny ability to judge character. She was always a tough woman, but that toughness sprang from an unflinching realism about human nature. The hardships she endured in childhood led her, for better and worse, to see things in black and white. She wasn't about to raise children who behaved like "that element."

That might sound elitist today, but there's something deeper at work here. Like all good Southern women, Mama believed in the secret power of manners—that they are the great leveler of social class. Good manners have the power to ennoble a poor man; they enable all who possess them to become, in the Southern writer Florence King's phrase, "aristocrats of the spirit." They are the means and proof of grace. And grace my mother had in spades.

William Alexander Percy, a turn-of-the-century Mississippi writer, wrote that "manners are essential and essentially morals"—a neat summation of Mama's philosophy of life. It would have been nearly impossible for my mother to separate a neighbor's code of manners from the quality of his character, the state of his soul. To her, crude or indifferent manners were not simply a matter of ignorance; they were a signal to the world that you were dishonorable, uncouth. Good manners, on the other hand, made social discourse pleasant under the best circumstances, and possible under the worst.

As with everything Southern, this devotion to social custom is steeped in history. "Rules of etiquette are not created—they are evolved," notes the 1890 edition of the *Blue Book of New Orleans*, a social registry. "The gentleness that marks modern social customs is the outcome of the wildest of passions." The bloody echoes of the Civil War, in particular, left Southern families grievously wounded in both body and spirit, investing future generations with a heightened sensitivity to feelings of wounded pride or humiliation. "War," the *Blue Book* observed, "the cruelest of sentiments, has given us every usage of etiquette which implies tender consideration for others, and makes modern social life more charming."

My friend Jill Conner Browne, the author of the *Sweet Potato Queens* books, has a simpler way of putting it: "Manners," she says, "are just the grease that keeps things running."

Even children of my generation were made sharply aware of the importance of manners, of their role as a moral compass to guide you through life. From our earliest years we were half-consciously aware of the discipline grown-ups showed around each other, and we knew we were expected to follow suit. Our parents, and the parents of our friends and neighbors, lived within well-defined boundaries of behavior. And as we grew older, and began holding our own in social settings like school and church, we came to recognize the practical value of manners. If you knew how to be courteous and considerate, it became apparent, you could enter into any social situation with confidence—and you were much more likely to get what you wanted. A charming manner, in other words, could often get you that second helping of pie.

In the time and place where we grew up—Mama was fortunate in this, I now realize—the wider community shared her demanding standards. It seemed as though everyone had agreed in advance on the basic rules governing children's behavior, and there was an unstated bond among adults to enforce those rules wherever a child might be. The South was one big in loco parentis zone. You didn't dare act up around strangers, because you knew a grown-up wouldn't hesitate to correct you. And you knew that if this stranger happened to tell your mama what you'd been doing, your mama would not only thank the stranger for caring enough to set you right, but see to it that you were punished when you got home.

I've since learned that the South didn't have a monopoly on this kind of thing. My husband, Howard, who grew up in Los Angeles, remembers in his childhood neighborhood parents calling a community meeting, gathering together to decide what to do about one troublemaking kid who was a bad influence on their children. The parents brought their complaints as one to the bad kid's parents, who were shamed into taking action to rein in their misfit son.

Try to imagine that happening today, anywhere. The kid's parents would hire a lawyer in a heartbeat. I wish the South were all that different, but I'm not sure it is, not anymore. A friend of mine who teaches sixth grade in a small Southern town tells me she pines for the days of our youth, when teachers and other adult authority figures were assumed to be in the right unless proven otherwise. Nowadays, when she calls a student's parents in to discuss a problem, more often than not they show up indignant, demanding that the teacher prove the case against their innocent angel.

"You see how this younger generation reacts to everything?" Daddy said the other day. "It's all about *me, me, me.*" And I hate to sound like an old fogy, but I can't help thinking he's right. There was more true freedom for kids when authority was respected, and a just order was in place. Manners are all about creating a society in which people can feel safe. If you grew up in it, you never lose your craving for that feeling of security. To some, Southern manners may seem quaint, even archaic. But I wonder if anyone really prefers the selfishness and crudity we see in so much of life today.

The geography of my childhood is mapped in the streets and yards of a green little enclave called Lakemont. Carved out of a beautiful old 1920s recreational area called Echo Park, Lakemont was a perfect natural habitat for the packs of wild young baby boomers who would soon be prowling its crew-cut lawns. My parents had settled there comfortably in 1954, moving first into a single-story ranch house, and then into a new brick-face split-level next door. The houses were tucked away at the end of a cul-de-sac with a few other sparkling new flat-roofed modernist homes—which, to anybody who was looking, might have revealed something about their inhabitants. My father was one of a loose collection of engineers and architects who'd entered the Meridian workforce at about the same time, and in the postwar years a handful of them colonized this little corner of Lakemont, just a stone's throw away from their offices on the main road.

On the surface it may have seemed like a typical suburban subdivision, but there was something about the connection among these families that gave the place a sense of real community. "We all knew each other," Daddy remembers. "Had the same background, education, worked on the same jobs." They all seemed to have so much fun together. I remember the weekly card games my parents and our neighbors took turns hosting: our house would fill with friends and laughter, the men arguing philosophically as the evening grew late. Mama always knew just the right thing to say; I marveled at her natural social graces, and wondered how I would ever learn what she knew.

There were no mountains in Lakemont, just hills. But there were two small lakes—ponds, really—and in the spring and summer they became weekend gathering places for the entire neighborhood. Like most people, when I recall my childhood what I am usually remembering are the weekends—warm and breezy, they all seemed to be, and spent in a blur of tireless activity and blissfully uninterrupted leisure. So many afternoons I spent sitting on the bank of one of the lakes, with a cane pole in my hand, waiting for a bream to take the worm on the hook. The little red and white plastic cork would disappear under the water, and I'd give the pole a little upward tug, and haul in the fish, as big as Daddy's hand. You'd see everybody there, Aunt Sara and Uncle Boots and neighbors and friends, with their coolers and lawn chairs and picnic lunches, talking and fishing, fishing and talking. When they drained one of the lakes, everybody— and I mean everybody—came to catch and eat the fish. It was like a communal feast. This was not in the country, mind you, but in the heart of a modern subdivision. Most of the men and women who lived there were Depression kids like my parents, and they weren't about to let those fish go to waste. Besides, there isn't a Southerner alive who doesn't love fried fish fillets.

Nowadays the neighborhood has aged, and there aren't many kids around. The levee we played on isn't often busy anymore, but I like to think that somewhere Mississippi children are still doing some lazy cane-pole fishing on a Sunday afternoon, not wasting their day in the mall or in front of a computer screen.

Not far from the lakes were a few scattered remnants of Echo Park, which for us children retained the mysterious aura of things long gone. By the time of my childhood they were largely grown over with brush, but you could still see the entrance to the concrete cave that had once been home to a bear named Chubby. CHUBBY BEAR'S CAVE, as the faded lettering still reads, was a neighborhood landmark; we'd crawl in, casting flashlight beams into dark corners to make sure no snakes were lurking, and then we'd scare ourselves to death holding miniature séances by candlelight. There was a persimmon tree hanging over the entrance to the cave, and when the fruits were ripe, we'd collect them as they fell. There were blackberry briars along the roadside by the cave, and we'd stain our hands purple picking the ripe ones.

When we weren't gathered around the lake with Mama and Daddy, we kids loved playing in the woods behind our house. Jenna, Berry, Brock, and I would build forts, sweeping the ground bare so we'd have soft dirt floors. We'd cut trails through the woods, and Berry would hunt birds with his BB gun. When somebody told him you could catch a bird if you put salt on its tail, he came up with a scheme in which he'd take a fishing pole with a purple plastic worm dangling on the end, dip the worm in salt, and try to touch birds' tails with the worm. I don't think the Lakemont birds were ever in danger.

Our neighborhood had a tennis court, and a swimming pool, where you'd see all your friends every day in the summer. There was an annual Lakemont picnic, with a potluck lunch spread three tables long, and all of those simple, old-fashioned games—sack races, bobbing for apples. When we weren't in the park itself we'd play flag football and whiffle ball in nearby fields with our pals, ride our bikes up and down the streets, spend the night at each other's houses, and do all the things neighborhood kids did in the days before the invention of the scheduled play date. The only rule was to be home for supper before dark.

On a summer night there was no better adventure than to stay over with my grandmother Annie Raye, the only one of my grandparents to survive into my childhood. She didn't have much money, and until her last years (when she moved in with us), she lived in a small apartment in a housing project in town. She smoked cigarillos, and read magazines like *Movie Mirror* and *True Detective Stories* with boundless appetite. I was never allowed to have coffee at home, but Grandma was always glad to sneak me a cup; she and I would sit at her little kitchen table, share a pot of coffee, and start our day together. I'd watch her forever, embroidering doilies and pillow-cases, or working away at the old-fashioned, pedal-driven Singer sewing machine in her apartment. (I'm having all the little things she embroidered cut up and reassembled as a keepsake quilt for her namesake, my daughter, Anabella Raye.) I miss the hum of the oscillating fan at the foot of her bed; at night it would fill that quiet apartment and lull me to sleep.

My grandmother was also a wonderful cook. She made the most delicious fudge, dense and thick and rich. I've never had any like it since she died. She wrote the recipe down, but Mama always said she must have left an ingredient out, because it's never turned out quite the way it should. She also made *the* best corn-bread dressing for the holidays. The other day my Aunt Nancy and I were remembering her leaning up against the stove on that crutch of hers, her long cigarillo hanging out precariously over the stovetop. "If you're looking for a missing ingredient," Nancy says, laughing, "you better think about that cigarette ash."

I was by nature a bashful child, and I rarely felt more secure and at home in the world than when I'd go into my grandmother's backyard, climb up into the mimosa tree, with its fuzzy blossoms the color of pink lemonade, and talk to it. I don't remember what I said to the tree, and it doesn't matter anyway. The important thing is that I felt the tree listened and understood me, achingly timid as I was, too fearful to pour out my heart to a living soul.

But I wasn't melancholy all the time. Most days I was happy to go look for something exciting to do. And I didn't usually have to look too far, because my father was always bringing something home that was way too much for us to handle. Once he gave my seven-year-old brother Berry a go-cart that must have gone twenty-five miles an hour; Mama almost had a heart attack watching Berry whipping around the driveway, his little head just barely visible over the steering wheel. On Saturday mornings we'd pile into the car and Daddy would take us chasing trains from intersection to intersection, blowing the horn and waving to the conductor.

If that sounds a tad dangerous, consider the other harebrained way we passed the time: chasing the bug truck. In the summer, the city would send a truck equipped with an insecticide fogger around town, spraying for mosquitoes. As soon as we heard the "fog machine" coming we'd go chasing it down the street, playing in the sweet-smelling cloud of insecticide smoke it left in its wake. It was probably aerosolized DDT, and it's a wonder we haven't all dropped dead of lung cancer. But, I'll admit it sure was fun at the time.

Home—that blessed word, which
opens to the human heart the most
perfect glimpse of Heaven, and helps to
carry it thither, as on an angel's wings.

—Lydia Child, 1843

2 ॐ

In my memories of childhood, time itself seems to stand still. The very quality of time, and of its passing, felt different in those days. And if it seems now that there was a sacredness to it, a sense that it was something not to be mastered but to relish with honest joy, perhaps it's no surprise that my mind wanders to my youthful memories of Sunday.

Christians and Jews alike observe the Sabbath as a day of rest, when men and women of faith step back from their everyday pursuits. It's a time to enjoy the God-given fruits of those labors, but also a time to rest in honor of something greater than ourselves and our immediate desires. A great rabbi, Abraham Joshua Heschel, put it this way:

The meaning of the Sabbath is to celebrate time rather than space. Six days a week we live under the tyranny of things of space; on the Sabbath, we try to become attuned to holiness in time. It is a day on which we are called upon to share in what is eternal in time, to turn from the results of creation to the mystery of creation, from the world of creation to the creation of the world.

Now, we Wards wouldn't have thought to put it that way, but we would have known what the rabbi meant. This is just how we felt about the Christian Sabbath. There was something special about Sunday—something that included God, certainly, but that also embraced the comforts of food and family.

Sometimes on those childhood Sundays I would wake up early, and find Daddy reading the paper at daylight; soft swing music wafted in from Mama's kitchen with the smell of breakfast. Everything was quiet and peaceful, and our house never felt more like home. After breakfast, Mama would dress us for church. Boys wore slacks, and coats and ties if they were older. Girls, like their mothers, would die a thousand deaths before showing up in pants. It was, plain and simple, a matter of respect for God. My sense is that dressing up for church taught us kids how important God was, well before we were able to understand theology. Even today I'm still a little bit scandalized by the thought that people who meet business clients in their nicest clothes will wear any old thing to church.

It was important for Daddy that we have religious instruction.

He had been raised Methodist, but his particular church was fire-and-brimstone fundamentalist. He had been disillusioned at an early age by a hypocritical preacher, and though he never lost his faith, he had a strong dislike for the kind of rigid Christianity Southerners call hard-shell. Still, that was part of his background, and he never could quite shake it. When I was a young child, an adult heard me call one of my brothers a fool, and told Daddy about it. Daddy took me aside and gave me a stern lecture about how the Bible says I could go to hell for that. It was strange hearing something like that coming from a man who disdained that kind of literal-minded religion.

Because the Bible Belt runs through the South, and Evangelical Protestantism is dominant there, many people assume Southerners are humorless about religion. But in truth, our appreciation for human frailty tends to make us more skeptical of hard-shell preachers and strict religion than we're given credit for. There's an old Southern joke that goes like this: If you're planning a fishing trip with a Southern Baptist, be sure to find another one to come along—one Baptist will drink all your beer, but if you have two to keep an eye on each other, neither one will touch the stuff. Another joke says that Southern Baptists don't like to fool around in bed, because they're afraid it could lead to dancing. Of course, the Baptists weren't above having a little fun themselves—usually at the expense of the worldly, upper-class Episcopalians (Whiskypalians, they called them) or the dour, "respectable" Presbyterians, whom Baptists call the Frozen Chosen.

My friend Becky tells a story about the last day she and her family were Baptists. One day, her husband dropped her and the children off in front of their church while he went to park the car.

"Next thing you know, there was Channel 3 News shoving a microphone in my face, asking me what do I think about the fact that our pastor had been caught soliciting for prostitution at some family seafood restaurant!" she says. "Well, I never! I said, 'You are kidding me!' And then—*haw!*—he did the worst thing. Instead of saying, 'I have sinned, please forgive me,' he told the congregation he'd been down there trying to bring the Gospel to fallen women. You know, 'Jesus meets the woman at the well.'

"My Lord, we were so humiliated," Becky says, laughing. "At that point, my husband said there must be something in the Baptist coffee that makes 'em crazy. So we finally changed to Presbyterian, so at least now I can have a decent drink if I feel like it."

In the South, it isn't so important which religion you subscribe to, as long as you're religious in some way. Southern people say grace at meals, and they talk about God more openly, and less self-consciously, than most other Americans. I've always felt ambivalent about that. I love how unashamed Southern folks are of their faith, but it can be off-putting if it's overdone. Proselytizing bothers me, and I don't like to hear people go on about their religion with pride in their voices. Maybe this is a legacy of Daddy's mistrust of preachers. Or maybe it's just that I believe religion is, at its heart, a private thing, and that you can tell those who are really holy by their humility.

The Ward children attended First Christian Church in downtown Meridian, and we always sat in the balcony (probably so Mama wouldn't be embarrassed if any of us acted up). I loved that church so much; I've spent all my life trying to find a place that makes me feel so warm, and so close to God. The handsome stone building was built in the 1920s by men who drove their Model T's out south of town to a rocky hillside, loaded the cars with the dark brown fieldstones, and ferried them back to the city for the stonemasons. Its interior was graced by simple but grand wooden Gothic arches, and during my childhood the walls suggested clotted cream; now they've been painted a delicate pink, but the carpet remains the color of ripe plums. The bright red doors, we were told, represented the fire of faith, but they seemed closer to the color of an old-style London phone booth. It was an uplifting, memorable space, filled on Easter with lilies and soft, natural light.

But what made it so captivating to me was the pastor, Dr. William Apperson. He was tall and Cary Grant handsome, and spoke with compassionate authority. He had been educated at Oxford, and his sermons were always filled with the words of men of learning: Shakespeare, Thoreau, Thomas Wolfe, the Romantic poets. Dr. Apperson, who died a few years ago, was a man of formality and dignity. In the 1960s, when ladies' skirts started creeping up above the knee, he had a short curtain installed above the front wall of the balcony, to prevent anyone from seeing something they shouldn't. He was a kind and gentle man; Mama always said he added such elegance to the church. I'm sure that the sense I've always had of God being a loving father comes from being around him and our church, which held me, a quiet, shy child, in its comforting embrace.

The gentle faith that was passed on to me at First Christian Church required only a general belief in the authority of the Bible, a conviction that you had direct access to God, and a commitment to love the Lord your God with all your heart, and love your neighbor as yourself. The church wasn't steeped in liturgy, but going there week after week, and doing the same plain things over and over again, took on the power of ritual in my imagination. Just as vivid are my memories of the pancake breakfasts we'd have once a year, and the taste of the foamy hot chocolate we kids would drink in the rec room before going out for an evening of Christmas caroling. Our church may have been downtown, but in every way that mattered it was an extension of home.

Despite the security and assurance I took from Sunday morning church, though, I also had a troubling sense that God was a stern, judging deity—that I had disappointed him in some vague, but very real, way, and that someday I might be punished for it. To this day I have no clear idea where that came from. It may well have been bolstered by my father's quiet authority, but I can't help feeling I must have absorbed it from the wider Southern culture, dwelling as it does on sin and alienation from God. Mindful of Southerners' anguished guilt at the vast distance between God and their fallen selves, Flannery O'Connor described the South as "Christ-haunted." If there is one regrettable legacy of Southern childhood, it may be that: a lingering, unshakable sense of shame.

After Dr. Apperson sent the congregation forth with his usual blessing, we'd often do what half of Meridian did for dinner, as the noonday meal is called in the South ("supper" is what you eat at night). We'd go to Weidmann's. Founded five years after the Civil War, Weidmann's is one of the oldest restaurants in the South. Its half-timbered façade is meant to suggest a Black Forest hunting lodge, but it's really a simple venue for reliable home cooking, served family style.

In my childhood, going back to Weidmann's—like stopping off at Aunt Margaret's—was literally like stepping back in time. The only sign that you were in the 1960s were the seasonal sports schedules for various Mississippi college teams posted on the wall. At the center of the restaurant were two cavernous rooms, the front one boasting a long lunch counter with red leather stools, the back one equipped with a horseshoe bar. Ceiling fans turn lazily overhead, not so much circulating the air as bumping it along. Stuffed and mounted heads of whitetail bucks and wild boars stare down from the dark paneled walls with the same cloudy eyes that have observed five generations of townspeople grow up on fried chicken, green beans, and black-bottom pie.

Whenever somebody who was anybody came through Meridian, they'd eat at Weidmann's—and if the owners could coax a publicity photograph out of them, it went up on the wall. The boxer Jack Dempsey came through several times in the 1940s, and left behind signed photos. John Stennis, Mississippi's legendary U.S. senator, is long gone from this world, but his stern glare was a fixture in the Weidmann's firmament. Hometown boy Jimmie Rodgers, the "Singing Brakeman" and the father of country music, was there; so was baseball great Dizzy Dean, and actor Vincent Price, who ate at Weidmann's while performing in Meridian in 1973.

There were countless yellowing photographs of big-haired Mississippi beauty queens and stump-necked Mississippi football players. The Hager Brothers, twins who found country-music fame on

Hee Haw in the 1970s, left an autographed photo. Who remembers the Hagers today? Weidmann's does. A photo of a middle-aged Dale Evans showed her sporting a bouffant so high it must have tickled the noses of the stuffed deer heads in Weidmann's dining room. And for every recognizable face there were dozens of other photos, each capturing some bathing beauty or glossy-haired swell who passed through, but whose signatures had long since faded to illegibility, their names lost to time and memory.

To my young imagination, Weidmann's was like a living museum of Mississippi history, those photographs marking time and endurance like rings on a venerable tree. Behind the lunch counter was a shot of Merrehope, the only antebellum mansion in Meridian to survive Sherman's fiery march through the Confederate heartland. The state champion 1942 Meridian High School Concert Band was memorialized on another wall. It was the kind of place local folks came to because, well, that's what people always have done.

One morning not too long ago I stopped by Weidmann's for lunch with a friend. The first thing our waitress, Dee, said was, "How's your mama?"

"Hanging in there," I said.

A moment later Jimmy, one of the young waiters, came over to ask the same thing, and I offered the same response. "Well, that's about all you can ask for," he said sweetly. He came back a few minutes later with a sack of cracklin bread. "I know your mama loves her cracklin bread. Take this home to her. And tell her I asked about her."

That day I ate my fill of corn bread, lima beans, black-eyed peas, and, of course, turnip greens. With the possible exception of grits, there's no food more Southern than greens, whose bitter smell while cooking down in salty fatback amid the jittery hiss of a pressure cooker is a Proustian madeleine for generations of black and white Southerners alike. The smell and taste of greens resonate particularly with men and women of my parents' generation, for whom many a Depression-era supper was made of greens, corn bread, and buttermilk. There's nothing like taking a slab of corn bread and sopping up the pot liquor from a mess of greens—whether turnip or collards, their harsher cousin.

One of the blessings of traditional Southern cuisine is how it has come to serve as a vehicle of communion between blacks and whites when they meet outside the South. It's something for which the late writer and editor Willie Morris, an expatriate Mississippian living in New York, was grateful. In his memoir *North Toward Home*, Morris describes bringing his wife up to the Harlem apartment of the jazz writer Albert Murray and his wife for dinner on New Year's Day 1967. They were joined there by novelist Ralph Ellison and his wife, and together the six Southerners, four black and two white, had what Morris described as "an unusual feast: bourbon, collard greens, black-eyed peas, ham-hocks, and corn bread—a kind of ritual for all of us. Where else in the East but in Harlem could a Southern white boy greet the New Year with the good-luck food he had had as a child, and feel at home as he seldom thought he could in [New York]?"

If the classic Southern comfort food hasn't changed at Weidmann's, in recent years something else has: It used to be a lot busier. When I was growing up, Weidmann's was a destination restaurant. They flew in fresh seafood from the Gulf of Mexico on a regular basis, including oysters straight from New Orleans. It was said to be

Alabama football coach Bear Bryant's favorite place to eat, which itself gave the place semireligious status. Back then, the din of dishes and silverware clanking on tables and pans banging in the kitchen was so loud we children could hardly hear ourselves think. It was so exciting. I remember sitting there in my Sunday dress, thinking Weidmann's was the center of the social universe—which, in Meridian, it was. Each table had a handmade clay jar of peanut butter in the center, and we kids would smear gobs of it on saltines while waiting for our food to come, causing Mama to fuss that we were ruining our appetites. Of course, she was right. I don't think any of us ever managed to finish our dinner. Still, I remember eating lots of fried chicken, crabmeat cocktail, shrimp remoulade, and that black-bottom pie, with its creamy chocolate filling and chocolate wafer crust.

While Daddy was settling the bill at the cash register, we kids would go trawling through Jean's Treasure Chest, a suitcase-sized box of candy set out for children to have a treat before they left. Not long ago, Jenna, Berry, and I were laughing over how puny the Treasure Chest really is. When we were kids, it could have fallen off a Spanish galleon as far as we were concerned.

After dinner, Daddy would often load us into the car and drive down to Enterprise to visit family. We loved hearing Daddy tell stories about his childhood days at Homeward—explaining why the house was built with a breezeway (or "dog trot," as it was called), how the old wooden stove worked, how they used to sleep in deep

featherbeds—things like that. And we'd always come home with a stash of jellies, preserves, pickles, and relishes from Aunt Margaret's pantry. But we were restless kids, and before long we'd start thinking about heading home, getting back to playing out, as we used to call it, with our neighborhood friends.

And that mix of restlessness and contentment certainly carried through to Christmastime. We had a few of our own twists on the traditional family Christmas—the first being that it always seemed to start at four o'clock in the morning on December 25. Each of us kids was assigned a particular piece of living room furniture, marked by our own personal Christmas stocking—as the oldest, I got the couch—and we would tumble together into the living room at the appointed hour and make a beeline for the stocking and unwrapped presents we knew that Santa had piled there for us to find.

But the real celebration came later that day, at the family Christmas party at Uncle Thomas Ward's place. All our big family events in those years were held in the dark-paneled living room of the big, stately home he shared with Aunt Carolyn and their three kids, Tom, Robert, and Judy. The whole clan—including Daddy's two sisters and their families—would gather there around dark on Christmas Day. I can close my eyes now and hear the tinkle of ice cubes at cocktail time, smell the sweet aroma of bourbon melting into the spicy scent of the cedar tree, and slip into a Yuletide reverie.

Though my own home in Los Angeles is decorated in a modern, minimalist style, the rich interior of Uncle Thomas's house remains my touchstone for what home looks and feels like. His house conveyed a sense of comfort, certainly, but it was a comfort that went beyond simple physical convenience. The furnishings and décor gave it a sense of security and solidity; they stood for tradition, as if the people who lived there must be in touch with an older, more civilized way of life. And the early memory of those warm family gatherings imprinted itself, I realize now, deeply upon my consciousness.

I recently had a *eureka!* moment while reading *Home*, a fascinating history of domestic life by the architect Witold Rybczynski. In the opening chapter Rybczynski examines the success of the designer Ralph Lauren, who has made himself the standard-bearer of a romanticized American classicism in style. (I often describe the atmosphere at Uncle Thomas's house as "like a Ralph Lauren ad," and most people know exactly what I mean.) Lauren excels at "evoking the atmosphere of traditional hominess and solid domesticity that is associated with the past," Rybczynski observes. "Is it simply a curious anachronism, this desire for tradition, or is it a reflection of a deeper dissatisfaction with the surroundings that our modern world has created? What are we missing that we look so hard for in the past?"

What, indeed? I can think of a hundred things: a sense of belonging, a sense of rootedness, a sense that our world is enduring and that we ourselves will endure along with it, through generation after generation. That is why, though I've never lived there myself, I'm glad that Homeward still stands today, and that my Aunt Celeste still lives there. It's why I'm glad my siblings and I have always remained close, far-flung though we may be. And maybe it's why I find my mind wandering back, these days, to those Christmases we spent together as children, in front of a warm fire, when all was right with the world.

❦ ·············· ❦

Many a night in those preteenage years, Jenna and I sat home with Mama, watching old movies starring beautiful women like Ava Gardner and Elizabeth Taylor, with their dark hair and dramatic makeup. That standard of beauty was really taken to heart by our parents' generation, especially in the South. There was lots of pressure to look perfect, and to *be* perfect—to live up to the unreachable ideal of womanhood. I remember Mama telling me when Jenna and I were really little that in our next house she wanted a staircase, so that when we were older she could watch us girls descend in our ball gowns as we left for a spring dance. And I think it must have been

Clowning around with Jenna.

from those old movies that Mama got her idea that if her daughters were going to become proper Southern ladies, they might need a little help.

When I was three, Mama sent me off to start taking dance lessons. I must have been feeling a need to be noticed, to stand out from the crowd. I remember performing in a revue as one of twenty little girls in a row, all dressed as miniature brides. All of a sudden— and much to my parents' alarm—I stepped out of line, marched front and center, and performed my routine solo. It seems I had the performer's showboating instinct from the beginning, though it would lie dormant for years.

My dance teacher was a local legend named Miss Mary Alpha Johnson. But dance wasn't the only thing she taught. Reader, I tell you proudly that I am a graduate of Miss Mary Alpha's charm school, where we aspiring ladies were instructed in the proper ways to walk, talk, sit, and behave.

We laugh at the idea of a charm school today, but I credit Miss Mary Alpha with teaching me poise and how to carry myself. In fact, it was so important to Mama that Jenna and I grow up to be proper Southern ladies that she enrolled us in a second charm school, a weeklong course at the Sears department store. Sears gave us a little textbook to study, filled with chapter titles like "Good Grooming Is Just a Matter of Organization."

I paid Miss Mary Alpha a visit on a recent trip home, and she entertained me graciously in her enchanting parlor, which is a little girl's fantasia of femininity. The walls are blush pink, the white trim looks like icing on a wedding cake, and the porcelain statues of ballerinas resemble spun sugar. A lady to her fingertips, she was wearing heels and jewelry, her white hair brushed up from her fine-boned, still-beautiful face like a swirl of meringue. That day Miss Mary Alpha was opening registration for a new class of dancers, as well as students for her charm school, but she still made time for me. We had pink fruit punch and homemade cheese straws, and talked of old times.

Is charm school dated? Well, I guess so. But if there were one available in Los Angeles, when the time came I would have my daughter, Anabella, enroll in a heartbeat. Social grace will never go out of style.

After leaving elementary school, I briefly attended public junior high before transferring to Lamar, a small, traditional private school. Starting in the ninth grade, the kids of the town were encouraged to join one of the same-sex social service clubs, which were like junior sororities and fraternities. The girls could join the Debs, Mes Amies, or the Dusties. I was a Dusty. The boys had Phi Kappa or DeMolay to choose from. Phi Kappa had chapters statewide. I was a Phi Kappa little sister, so I would get to go to a lot of conventions and chapter meetings in towns all over the state, which were full of eligible boys. Needless to say, it was a blast. All the local social clubs had a dance every year that was known as a "lead-out." Girls dressed in long gowns to be formally announced; sporting black tie, their dates would escort them to the front of a stage to have their photograph taken, then we'd go home and change into pants for the dance.

These clubs were the center of our high school social life, and if you didn't belong to one, you were relegated to the margins. The pressure to conform, and the fear of not belonging, was so great that most kids were willing to put up with sadistic hazing during the pledge period, which not for nothing was called Hell Week. For the girls the ordeal was purely emotional, but the boys had to suffer physical abuse, too. It was pretty cruel, actually.

If you were a girl suffering through Hell Week, you weren't allowed to shave your legs. You weren't allowed to drive—you had to ride your bicycle everywhere. You couldn't see a guy. (I got "caught" once when a boy I was friendly with stopped by, for a completely innocent visit; I leapt into bed to pretend sickness, and narrowly escaped censure.) You'd have to deliver small gifts, called "happies," to older members of the club. If you'd run into a member during that week, you'd have to perform a charming little move called an "air raid," which involved falling immediately to the ground and reciting something you'd been told to memorize. I remember having to commit to memory, among other things, the lyrics to "Sweet Baby James" by James Taylor. And during Hell Night, the culmination of it all, the older girls would scream at you, crack eggs over your head, make you write essays on toilet paper— anything to force their will upon you.

But for me those humiliations were just a start. Two of the girls, Cheri and Sally, decided they would make me wear a sign everywhere that said I'M BEAUTIFUL AND I KNOW IT. I was an extremely self-conscious fourteen-year-old, and have never felt more vulnerable. I'd never given too much thought to how I looked, and I was far too shy and insecure to be conceited. But that's not how the other girls saw me. They didn't even know me, but they were determined to take me down a peg.

Walking around with that poster board sign hanging around my neck for a week was perhaps the most scarring experience of my young life. I allowed these girls, whose adolescent envy, self-doubt, and insecurity were at high tide, to humiliate me in order to bolster their own fragile self-image. Worse yet, I allowed them to do it because I so wanted to belong to their club. I let them make me wear a sign that made me seem haughty and arrogant, knowing it was intended to publicly cancel out whatever physical beauty I possessed. They believed that everything came easy to me, and by God, they were going to rob me of that.

At the age of fourteen, it truly felt as if they were murdering my soul. Even now, all these years later, I don't think that's an exaggeration. I remember feeling so confused, convinced I must have deserved that kind of treatment—that I was so worthless it only made sense for the other girls to treat me that way. These girls were troubled, I now see, and they had to cut me down to size to alleviate their own feelings of inadequacy. With the passage of time, of course, we find ways to explain such things away, and even forgive them. But the mark they make on us is indelible.

It took me years to get over the pain and doubt inflicted upon me in that solitary week of humiliation. Every time I would accomplish something that had anything to do with my physical appearance—becoming a cheerleader, being elected Homecoming Queen in college, becoming a model—I would be racked by self-doubt, haunted by the worry that I was a hollow person with nothing to offer but an attractive façade. All because of a culture—a culture especially prized in the South, I realize—that made a contest, and a currency, of adolescent beauty, and in the process turned generations of young women against one another. And I endured it without complaint, just to belong.

Once you were in one of these clubs, of course, it was all peaches and cream. We went to chapter meetings, did community-spirited things such as visiting the elderly at rest homes or helping out at children's shelters. The lasting legacy for me, though, was the meanness I had to endure to get in. If social cohesion is one of the good things about growing up in a small town, the downside is the unchallengeable power of cliques. That sort of thing is in the nature of the teenage beast, but in bigger towns and cities there are usually so many different social groups within a single school or locality that most kids can find others they feel comfortable with. Not so in a small town. If you don't conform, even at the cost of sacrificing your principles and self-respect, you will be an outcast. And if you have a sensitive nature, it will mark you for life.

Many years later I ran into Sally, one of the girls who had been so mean to me during Hell Week, at a class reunion back home. I decided to talk to her about what she had done to me, hoping it would help me come to terms with my own memories. She was horrified. The next day she sent me an arrangement of flowers, in the colors of the Dusties. The card said, "You're beautiful, and *I* know it." It was such an elegant and gracious thing to have done, and I was so glad I'd taken the risk of approaching her. It made it possible to build a lovely friendship with Sally, rather than continue to mourn that one horrible week when we were teenagers. I think we're both grateful that we found a way to forgive and be forgiven.

There were only thirty-five kids in my graduating class, so everybody knew everybody else at Lamar. I never went steady in high school, just dated a bunch of different guys. We'd go water-skiing a lot, and to the movies, and ball games, or go tubing down the Chunky River. In the summer we'd have lake-house parties in nearby locales, or go for big weekend jaunts to New Orleans. Music was a big part of our life; we drove to Mobile, Tuscaloosa, and Jackson for concerts as our favorite bands toured through the South. But our most common pastime was to hang out in the parking lot of the Quik Stop—and that was as much fun as anything.

Sandy Steele was my best friend then, and I did everything with her and three other girls. After I got my license we'd all pile into the red Plymouth Barracuda Daddy bought me, and drive around the houses of boys we had crushes on. We'd slow down, hoping to catch sight of a boy out washing the car in his driveway—then we'd have a shrieking giggle fit, and floor it. That's small-town courtship for you.

This story would be a lot spicier if I could offer true confessions of a failed Southern lady. The truth is I was a good girl, more Melanie Wilkes than Scarlett O'Hara. I don't credit it to any particularly strong sense of virtue. Rather, it had to do with my chronic shyness, and the severe pressure to conform to my mother's and society's expectations.

I was the perfect young Southern woman: quiet, demure, feminine, seen and rarely heard. Polite. Proper. Never raised my voice, never gave my parents a moment's trouble. Shied away from unpleasantness. Strove to maintain that teeth-together-lips-apart ideal. And

With Dusties and others, posing at the Lamar homecoming.

I wouldn't have had the courage to risk a moment's presumption. I will never forget this: One day during my teenage years my next-door neighbor's mother, a sophisticated woman and family friend, took me aside. "Sela," she told me, "you must never think that you're beautiful. It's just not an attractive trait. There's always someone more attractive than you, and always someone less so." And I was my mother's daughter: I never doubted for a moment that she was right.

My Southern childhood was a happy time. And yet somehow, by the time I was through with high school, I had become overwhelmed by the urge to escape. Why was I so lonely? Why did I want to leave? Why was I afraid that if I didn't get out of town, some essential part of me would die, and I would never get over it?

On reflection, of course, what finally drove me away from the South was the very same code of customs and manners I look back on today with such wistful admiration. For better and for worse, Southern manners were the defining influences of my life. They made me love the South and hate it, too, sent me away as surely as they now draw me back.

What I was feeling, it's clear to me now, was a growing discomfort with the unforgiving rules of the old Southern social order. As a child I had lived within those rules as within a warm blanket, nurtured and protected by the sense of security they offered—but at a price. This culture of honor and chivalry, which defines Southern society and gives it so much of its decency and beauty, has a dark side, and that is shame.

Honor, after all, is something that can only be conferred by others. So if you're raised in a society obsessed with personal honor, you're likely to spend an awful lot of your life worrying about what others think of you. And more often than not you'll be willing to contort yourself to no end in order to save face, or to keep others from losing face.

Even as a little girl, I had a distant awareness of the costs of such behavior. Mama, for example, always insisted that we step aside and allow others to pass ahead of us. It was the decent thing to do, she said, and of course in principle she was right. And yet I've since learned that it's not always the best thing to let a pushy person get ahead of you in line—especially when you're as naturally shy or self-effacing as I was. The line between demurring from a position of strength, and doing so out of fear of causing a scene isn't always clear in such a rigid society.

You can imagine how crazy-making this can be. Southerners can be bizarrely averse to confrontation. Daddy and Mama once sustained a serious blow to their finances rather than force a showdown with a local advisor who left them exposed in a business deal. This isn't a matter of weak character. It would have involved accusing the man of negligence—which is to say, of being dishonorable. That's a cut that goes very deep down South, and it doesn't heal easily, if at all. A man can be ruined forever if he loses his honor. My folks must have figured that so unpleasant a confrontation wouldn't be worth the trouble—or perhaps that the kinder thing was to overlook the offense.

Southerners like my parents tend to embrace a fantasy image of perfection that will admit no flaw, weakness, or shortcoming. For them denial isn't just a coping mechanism; it's a way of life. When I was growing up, you'd hear ladies pronounce the name of serious diseases under their breath, as if whispering a word like "cancer" would somehow keep the affliction away. Things deemed unpleasant—menstruation and sexuality, but also grave matters such as unplanned pregnancy, wife-beating, or alcoholism—were spoken of only rarely. And if they were, the discussion was so smothered in euphemism and indirection that it made frank discussion next to impossible.

The silent suffering endured by so many Southerners, especially women, can only be guessed at. A friend of mine once told me about his ninety-four-year-old great-grandmother, who lived with her husband in a tiny Southern mill town during the Depression. She had to work as a telephone operator to help feed her family, which didn't go unnoticed among the other respectable women in the town. "The uppity ladies looked down on me, but I didn't let it get to me because I knew that they had nothing to be uppity about," he remembers her saying. "They carried on like aristocrats, but the truth was, their doctor and lawyer husbands were running around on them whenever their backs were turned. They knew it, and everybody else did, too. 'Course, you couldn't say anything about it."

No, you couldn't, because to talk about financial hardship or sexual infidelity would be to admit that there was something wrong with you. And that's not easy to do in the South. That old woman's husband probably felt shame that his family was so desperate that his wife had to go to work. But he never would have spoken about it—he just wouldn't have been able to.

What's at the bottom of all this, I can't help feeling, is fear—fear of vulnerability, of emotional need, of weakness of any kind. It calls to mind a memory that has stayed with me longer than I'd have expected: When we were children, Mama would drive us past the graveyard, and ask us, "Who's buried in that cemetery?"

"*Who?*" we'd say together, following the familiar ritual.

"Minnie!" Mama would say.

"Minnie *who?*"

"Minnie people!" she'd say, then cackle in a witch's voice.

"Mama, stop!" we'd yell. "Mama, *stop!*" But she'd just keep on laughing.

I remember that story because, as funny as it seemed, passing those headstones always *did* scare me a little, and I think it did her, too. That joke of Mama's was her version of whistling past the graveyard. She knew we were afraid of the unknown, of bad things happening, of what's under the ground—in other words, of what's not being said. She felt the need to protect us kids from the horror of death by making a macabre joke about it. Don't spend too much time dwelling on mysteries; don't upset the order of things. *Look away* from those unhappy thoughts. *Look away.*

And the truth is, I spent much of my childhood looking away. I've come to see that as one of the roots of my childhood loneliness. Was I exceptionally sensitive as a child? I don't know. I was an observant child, I know. But I spent so much time worrying about what was okay to say, what might be safe to ask—so much so that I only felt safe expressing myself in the branches of my grandmother's mimosa tree, or later at the cemetery, where I sat and opened my heart to David, the brother I never knew.

When it came to being in public, all I knew was that it was my duty always to look on the bright side of things, to keep up with the convivial bonhomie of the tight-knit community around me. And as the oldest child, somehow I knew it was my role to teach my sister and brothers to do the same. This was the difficult underside of my mother's insistence on decorum: From Daddy's drinking to my own fear of loneliness, so many things went unspoken, for fear of betraying the family trust. I was fitted early for that stoic mantle, and it rested heavy on my shoulders.

Despite Mama's best efforts to make me into Miss Magnolia Blossom, by the end of my high school years that deep, contrarian part of me—the Daddy's girl part—had begun to assert itself. I knew that if I stayed in Meridian, I'd spend my life worrying over the things I'd never had the chance to do, because they just weren't available in a small Southern town. I might have had a comfortable life, following the path that society laid out for young women like me. But it would have meant giving up on something—on the unknown, on the chance to ask those questions—and somehow I knew it. So I decided I would leave Meridian. I might come back someday, but if and when I did I would bring with me some knowledge of the outside world, some knowledge of myself and what I was capable of.

I finished high school a year early, and spent a year at a local junior college preparing for full-fledged university study. During that time I bought a Barron's guide to colleges, looking for the perfect school. Most of my friends were going off to Ole Miss or Mississippi State, but by then my teenage wanderlust was too strong. I deliberately chose an out-of-state school, just to meet new people. For whatever reason—probably having to do with my longing for tradition—I concluded that William and Mary, the oldest college in the South (and second oldest in the United States), was the place for me.

During my spring semester at junior college I sent off for an application to William and Mary, but it turned out they wouldn't be able to accept me until the following spring. What would I do for the fall semester? Spending it at Ole Miss or State was out of the question. I decided to give the University of Alabama a chance. One semester wouldn't be so bad, and it would help me get used to living away from home.

I told Mama and Daddy my plan, and they were content. But for me that summer passed too slowly. By now Meridian felt like a fish-bowl, and I squirmed with anticipation of leaving.

Finally, in the waning days of August 1974, I said goodbye to my fretful mama and my best friend, Jeanne, the only ones to see me off; my stoic daddy had gone down to our beach house for the weekend, doubtless shying away from an emotional goodbye. I cranked my red Barracuda, slipped Dan Fogelberg into the 8-track, set my compass for Tuscaloosa, and drove off alone, into my future.

A solitary sail that rises
While in the blue mist on the foam—
What is it in far lands it prizes?
What does it leave behind at home?

—Mikhail Lermontov

3 ◈

....

When I look back on it now, through the crystal lens of hindsight, it doesn't surprise me that I chose to leave Mississippi to go off to college in another state—that I left everything I knew, in search of a world I knew not at all. What does surprise me, as I think back on that ninety-minute northeasterly ramble across the Alabama border from Meridian to Tuscaloosa, is that I made the trip by myself. As I remember it, most kids who set off for college in my day hung on to their parents as long as they could—or at least long enough to help with the unpacking and share a few teary goodbyes outside the dormitory, before sending them back home with a lighter car and a heavier heart.

But the interior journey I was making, as I drove away from my home and my family, wasn't like that at all. Setting off alone the way I did made me feel like—well, maybe Lewis and Clark. I must have made it clear to Mama and Daddy that I was fine going off by myself, and in retrospect, I guess there was something deep within me telling me to try and cut those apron strings.

The whole idea of college must have seemed especially romantic to my generation of teenage girls, who read *Love Story* in high school. I'm not even sure I'd ever heard of the Ivy League before then; now, though, I spent days on end dreaming of studying at Radcliffe, which appeared so stylish and romantic to my seventeen-year-old mind. I even named my Barracuda after Ollie, the character played by Ryan O'Neal in the movie. It's strange today to realize how little thought I'd given to the world beyond my hometown. But America was a different place then; I suspect there were many people like my family, who just didn't spend much time worrying about what it might be like to live elsewhere. Today, thanks to the movies, TV, and the Internet, our kids grow up thinking of the whole country, maybe even the planet, as their own. My childhood world was a much smaller place.

From my first day of college onward, though, the University of Alabama gave me all the world I was ready to handle. My high school class had thirty-five students; now I was entering a campus of sixteen thousand. When I arrived on that first fall day, I knew only one solitary soul on campus—a girl named Neva, who'd also come from Meridian. When I think back to the soundtrack of my life then—dominated by melancholy singer-songwriters like Dan Fogelberg and Joni Mitchell—it seems as though this must have been a mournful, introspective time. But in truth what I remember was very

With my dear friend Jeanne Fort and our little group of artist friends.

little anxiety, and a tremendous amount of excitement. My worries (*How will I ever find my way around this campus?*) were incidental, and soon were swept away in a flush of excitement and pioneer spirit.

After a week or so in a dorm I didn't like at all, I tried to sneak in and live with Neva, but her roommate took great objection. Finally, though, I learned that the university had an honors dorm, and much to my delight my grades were good enough to get me in. Honors-dorm residents were eligible for certain coveted privileges—namely, that guys could come up for a visit. And before too long the idea of transferring to William and Mary after a year faded into nostalgia. In the haze of my memory, the rest of my freshman year at Bama is like one long evening spent lighting candles and playing Phoebe Snow, and in my more thoughtful moments wondering gleefully, *How on earth did I get here?*

I chose the University of Alabama largely on the recommendation of my high school art teacher, Mrs. Gilder, who had gone there herself. I had been serious about art since the seventh grade, when I was selected to take advanced painting and drawing classes. There's nothing like a dose of unsolicited approval to get a young girl motivated; I decided right then that I wanted to be a painter.

When I first arrived in Tuscaloosa, the art program was my primary focus. As far as I was concerned, the old buildings where the art classes were held—small French Quarter–like structures sheathed in wrought-iron filigree, and centered around lush courtyards—were the closest I was ever going to get to the ateliers of the nineteenth-century French Impressionists whose work I so loved. The air was fragrant with the heady smells of turpentine and paint, and I sailed through my classes in art history and figure drawing, carried along by gushing enthusiasm for the world of beauty that was opening up to me. The greater part of it was sheer excitement over painting itself, and the discovery of new artists (who may have been Old Masters, but were still new to me). But part of the enchantment of those days was meeting other people who shared my sensibilities and interests. For the first time, I began to believe that I wasn't such a square peg after all. Not only was I discovering and deepening my passion for art, I was making friends with young people who were a lot like me, many of them from small Southern towns, too.

For me, the intellectual and social thrill of all this was beyond anything I could have anticipated—though I realize now, with affection, that when it came to art, Tuscaloosa in the 1970s wasn't exactly fin de siècle Paris. But it felt that way to me back then, and it may have been all I could have withstood at the time. For in some meaningful ways—more meaningful than I knew at the time—the trip from Meridian to Tuscaloosa wasn't much of a trip at all.

In truth, the school I'd chosen was an extension of home. I wouldn't have any of my childhood beliefs challenged in a serious way at Alabama, as I might have at a Northern school. Of course, I was never going to be the stereotypical alienated artist, filled with contempt and disdain for tradition or commerciality. As engaged as I was by my art classes, the locus of my social life at the university was an institution designed to ensure the carrying on of traditions of all kinds: the Greek fraternity and sorority system.

Southerners treasure the clubbiness of the Greek lifestyle, the sense of importance given to social ritual—and it shows. Whether it's at Ole Miss, LSU, the University of Georgia, or Alabama, one of the most glorious sights on any Southern campus is the array of grand old homes that house the fraternities and sororities. And no block in Beverly Hills is as grand as Alabama's Sorority Row, a string of residences that can only be described as plantation homes without the plantation. The stately grandeur of these homes, and the effort made to keep them in decent repair despite the wear and tear of decades of student use and abuse, is a testament to their enduring memory in the hearts of the Greek alums who populate the upper reaches of Southern social and economic life.

When I left for college, I made sure to get there in time for rush, that short, intense period when aspiring fraternity or sorority members make the rounds of all the parties—ice-water teas, we called them—trying to find the right fit. One of the teas I attended was at Chi Omega, whose house was as big as a Mississippi riverboat, and filigreed with wrought-iron balconies just like a French Quarter town house. And when we started hearing back, it was Chi O whose bid I accepted. For the rest of my college days, my Chi O sisters would stand in for my family, offering me the warm and welcoming stability of a home away from home.

But it wasn't a perfect system, to be sure. There was something contrived about the hasty bonding of sorority sisters that didn't always sit right with me. And for all the apparent closeness we felt in the sorority house, if anyone there was harboring secrets, nobody really talked about them. If you suffered from an eating disorder or depression or anything that would make others think you were less than perfect, you never, ever brought it up. Now and then we'd hear a girl throwing up in the bathroom, and we'd know, but we pretended not to hear. A Southern lady didn't talk about such things.

In a world of twenty-four-hour Jerry Springer confessionals, it's easy to feel that people have grown all too ready to open up their private lives for public consumption. But there we were, a houseful of girls in this exciting yet vulnerable time in our lives, living together as a family, yet suffering silently, deathly afraid to air anything that resembled dirty laundry. Today, at least, a woman can address her problems openly, with friends, counselors, even family. But back then all that mattered was what was proper. Years after we graduated, one of my sorority sisters wrote me and revealed that she'd been sexually abused as a child. And when I think of her carrying that burden alone for so long, I'm glad that this is one old-school legacy my children won't share.

Along those lines, we didn't talk much about sex. Of course, we did spend plenty of time thinking about boys, as sorority sisters everywhere are prone to do. I remember driving around campus, thinking, *My husband is around here somewhere.* But this was 1974, and Alabama was a pretty conservative place. Remember Lynyrd Skynyrd's line from "Sweet Home Alabama": "Watergate doesn't bother me/Does your conscience bother you?" That pretty much described the atmosphere at the university. College campuses elsewhere might have been the sites of freewheeling, seventies-era sexuality, but for all practical purposes the sexual revolution hadn't yet arrived in Tuscaloosa.

The sorority environment was designed to prevent vice more than encourage virtue: there was always somebody watching over you. Kiss your date good night on the front porch, and you'd get slapped with a fine; God forbid the two of you should stay out all night together, for you'd return to find they'd put a chair in your bed on the sleeping porch, a signal of your wicked ways. When my Catholic suitemate Ginger and I began getting more involved with our first serious boyfriends, we stayed up late at night searching the Bible for clues about just how far we could go with them and still avoid the stain of sin. We were so earnest, so sweet—and so naive!

But the real key to social life in my college days wasn't dating—it was football. Oh, to be in Denny Stadium on a Saturday afternoon in the fall! Everyone dressed up, as fine as if they were going to church: the guys in jacket and sometimes tie, we girls in dresses. Families came from miles around to join their daughters at the sorority houses for lunch, and then we'd all walk ceremonially over to the stadium. The air would be crisp with autumn and anticipation. For the really big games, we all packed up and headed to Birmingham, which had a larger stadium to accommodate the overflow crowds. Cars and RVs streamed in from all over the state, decorated with crimson and white streamers, GO BAMA! scrawled in white shoe polish on the windows.

There was a festival air to these weekends, and for most of the folks who drove overnight to get there I think it was a kind of a pilgrimage, too. Football was like a religion for so many of us, not just in the South but all over the country, and of course today sports is one thing we all still have in common—whether you're rooting for the Dallas Cowboys, the Nebraska Cornhuskers, or the squad of local boys who scrimmage between the high school bleachers on Friday night.

The boys we were rooting for, of course, were the Crimson Tide. The Tide was a national powerhouse, and being a part of the

Alabama football program in the 1970s was like having a box seat at the eye of a hurricane. I'd always loved football; I'd been a cheerleader since forever, because that was the one way I could be a part of it all. And when I got to Alabama I somehow found the courage to try out for the varsity squad, and was lucky enough to be chosen. *Come on*, you're thinking, *it takes courage to try out for cheerleader?* In those days, at that school, yes, absolutely.

One of the reasons was coach Bear Bryant.

Throughout the South, Coach Bryant was revered in the 1970s as pretty much the second coming of Robert E. Lee. He won more games than any coach in college football history, but that wasn't really the reason. A child of sharecroppers, Paul Bryant had won a football scholarship to the University of Alabama, and when he returned to forge his winning career he became the best kind of hero—the country boy made good, who rose to the heights of national fame while remaining down-to-earth. Coach Bryant was stoic but feeling, plain but noble. To those of us who attended Alabama in those years he seemed to dwell on Mount Olympus. Yet everyone knew he was one of our own, and we loved him for it. He was as close to a secular saint as any Southerner is ever going to see. When he died in 1983, half a million people—half a million!—lined the road between Tuscaloosa, where his funeral was held, and Birmingham, where he was laid to rest.

I'll never forget the first time I met him. I had to go into his office all by myself to arrange a pep rally, and I was scared to death. But then he looked up at me and smiled. "If I'da known you were comin' ovah," he said, "I'da awduhed us up some frahd chicken." I melted. It was as if I'd had an audience with the pope.

With Bob Baumhower.

Another time, a fellow cheerleader and I timidly went up to him on the field, and he jokingly said, "You gulls, you only come t'see me because you wanna get yo' picture taken." He probably wasn't far off. Everyone who met him really wanted to connect with him somehow. He was a living legend. In the South we're especially romantic and history-conscious, so we're awfully good at creating these figures. But all across America we have them—favorite teachers, sports figures, even (sometimes) politicians we look to for inspiration. Somehow they help us to understand ourselves and each other; they tell us what home is.

My college sweetheart was Bob Baumhower, one of the star defensive linemen for the Tide. He was everything you could want in a first love: tall and handsome, kind and loving, a big old bear of an Alabama boy. He'd take me out to Lake Tuscaloosa for barbecues, picnics, and band parties, and we'd have sunset cruises on his family's boat. Now that I have a daughter of my own, I miss those innocent days, when it was okay for a girl to wait until college—when she was better able to handle herself emotionally—to lose her heart to her first real boyfriend. Today things move so fast for kids that it's hard to imagine most girls could get to college without having their hearts broken by a string of immature bad boys. I hope my Anabella is fortunate enough to have as her first love a fellow as caring and grounded as Bob. (And as handsome!)

On game days we cheerleaders would arrive at the stadium well before the game started, to get some practice in. Bob would be on the field warming up; we'd send flirtatious signals to each other on the sidelines, and I'd get all giddy with those butterfly love rushes. The big game, the roar of the crowd, the Million Dollar Band playing the fight song, my sweetheart in shoulder pads on the field next to me—I didn't think life could possibly be more exciting than that.

I didn't realize it at the time, but this was my first experience of show business. Most of the important games were televised nationally, and the cameramen never missed the opportunity to get a shot of the cheerleaders. Mama would call and say, "Oh, we saw you on TV!" We started getting fan mail from all over the country; a little posse of younger girls even started standing outside the stadium, waiting for our autographs as we left.

We cheerleaders weren't only attached to the football team. We traveled with the Alabama basketball squad, too. And one trip we took with them—to the National Invitational Tournament, held in New York's Madison Square Garden—would change my life forever. I'd been fascinated with the Manhattan skyline since seventh grade, when I first saw it in a photograph. New York City is frightening to a lot of small-town people, and back in the seventies there was good reason to be afraid of it. The jazzy metropolis of Cole Porter, Joe DiMaggio, and so many others had turned into a place of crime, filth, drugs, and chaos, and for every starry-eyed visitor like me there were plenty of born-and-bred New Yorkers who couldn't get out of the city fast enough.

But I couldn't see that, or at least I wouldn't. Sure, there were bums in the streets, hookers on the corners; but there were also fabulous street musicians busking for quarters (dollars if they were lucky), wide avenues choked with yellow cabs migrating uptown to spawn,

and energy, everywhere energy, as if the streets themselves were electric cables pulsing with life. Once there, I never wanted to leave. I loved it, just loved it. I'd never seen a place that seemed so exciting and so alive. I don't remember how Alabama did in that tournament; all I remember was making a vow to myself that someday I'd come back to live there. This skyscrapered island city, about as far away as you can get from bucolic Meridian, was calling me home—home to a place I'd never been.

Was it strange being an art major in this tempest of sorority life, football, and cheerleading? I certainly didn't think so at the time. I loved both; why should I give up one for the other? Yet at some point in my sophomore year, an art teacher asked me, "Do you really think you'll pursue art seriously?" I said yes at the time, but I began to wonder if it was true. At that time Pop Art was very much in vogue, and it dominated my classes at Bama. I wasn't drawn to its ironic, superficial style, and I began to worry that being out of lockstep with the art world would prevent me from doing anything as a professional painter. At some point that year, I decided practicality was the wiser choice, and expanded my major to include communications.

This turned out to be a shrewd move. The year before I graduated, ABC was exploring the idea of having a college-age woman do color commentary from the sidelines. Sportscaster Jim Lampley was covering a Bama game, and he asked if any of us cheerleaders were in the communications school. I was! This was my first big break. I was all of nineteen years old.

It turned out that Jim meant *broadcast* communications, which wasn't my area. But it didn't matter. ABC sent a twenty-four-year-old assistant producer to Tuscaloosa to tape me doing color pieces on campus. I must have done pretty well, because they sent the guy back a few months later to tape me summarizing the highlights of a basketball game. Trouble was, I didn't really care for basketball. Sure, I'd been a cheerleader for the Crimson Tide roundballers, but I was a one-sport girl—and football it was.

Still, what kind of fool would I have been to withdraw from the audition when it just might be my ticket to success, or some new world? The producer and I went to a Bama basketball game, and I just sat there with a blank legal pad on my lap. I was supposed to take notes so I could summarize the game from quarter to quarter. But I didn't know the difference between a pick-and-roll and a Pic 'N Save—and halfway through the game, the legal pad remained sadly blank.

The gallant young assistant producer saw my distress. "I'm not supposed to help you," he leaned over and whispered, "but I'm going to make some notes and you might want to glance over at them." His notes saved me: they gave me something to read—a script to memorize, you might say—even if I didn't have a clue what I was talking about. In the end, I didn't get the job; later it went to Phyllis George. But I kept in touch with the assistant producer after I graduated in 1977. We started dating after Bob moved on to play with the Miami Dolphins; he would fly in from New York to see me on the weekends, which I found glamorous and exciting. When Sundays rolled around, I so often wished I could get on the plane with him and move to the city of my dreams. And I did get there eventually—but not before a little detour. Just before I graduated, I was approached by a friend of Coach Bryant's, who owned a Pepsi-Cola distributor in Memphis. Some Birmingham advertising agency had told him what he really needed was a Pepsi Girl to start making personal appearances representing the drink at golf tournaments and the like. This guy practically hired me off the sidelines: after my "interview," which consisted of him taking me to some sort of Mardi Gras ball, he gave me a job in his public-relations department. I really think the guy just wanted a date, but he was a perfect gentleman, and I had my first job. I was twenty.

On my first day, the general manager showed me my desk. "You need any help," he said, "just let us know." Well, I had no idea what I was supposed to be doing, none at all. I was a fine-arts and advertising major; I never cracked a book in public relations. All I knew was that one of these days, I was going to have to show up at some damn golf tournament.

I called Mama. "You can always come home, Sela," she said. "Your friend Patti just got a job at AT&T, with all kinds of benefits. What you have is not a real job." Maybe Mama was right, but I wasn't about to come home for supper the first time I was called. So instead I went to the nearest college bookstore and bought a public-relations textbook. I'd hide it in my lap under my desk, reading it as if I were searching for the secret code that would tell me what I was supposed to be doing. I had my head down so much I bet my coworkers thought I was in a constant state of prayer—which, given my desperate straits, I might as well have been.

One day the general manager—a cocky young Yankee from Chicago—summoned me into his office. He looked grim.

"You know," he said, "I couldn't help noticing that you have Coca-Cola bottles all over the floor of your car."

Well, yeah. Good Southerners drink Coke. Everybody knows that. But here I was, about to lose my job over it.

"I'm so sorry," I said, then whispered, "I just hate the taste of Pepsi."

"Well, you've probably never drunk it on ice," he said. He filled a glass with ice cubes, opened a bottle of Pepsi, emptied it into the glass, and had me taste it.

"You know, that is a lot better," I lied. I knew I was sunk. And there was really nothing more for me to do there. I stayed for a month longer, then slunk away. I never did make it to a single golf tournament.

By now, I was out of patience waiting for my New York break. I applied to be a flight attendant, and Delta flew me to Atlanta for an interview. On the flight home I met a man who was with Jack Morton Productions, a Manhattan company that did synchronized slide presentations for corporate clients. When I mentioned I had a degree in fine arts, he started talking to me about a possible job drawing storyboards and producing audiovisual presentations as a freelancer. "If you ever move to New York, look us up, we'll give you a shot," he said.

At that point, this was all the encouragement I needed. With only the promise of a nice man I met on a plane, I became a New Yorker.

The man was as good as his word, and my arts degree earned me my first job in the city, making $6.50 an hour, illustrating concepts in pen and ink before they were put on film. As I quickly discovered, my salary would reduce me to near-poverty levels in Manhattan, the only place in the city where I could possibly consider living. I found a roommate and took a tiny apartment in the Andover, a building at Eighty-eighth Street and York Avenue on the Upper East Side. Nestled among the old working-class German and Hungarian parts of town, the Andover seemed worlds, not blocks, away from tony Park Avenue. But I didn't care. After all, I was still writing home to Mama for help paying the bills; I knew I ought to make some kind of sacrifice—particularly since she wasn't exactly comfortable with my move in the first place.

"Why, Sela, *why?*" Mama protested when I told her I was moving to the city. "Why, of all the places in the United States, would anybody choose to live and work in New York City?" To many Southerners, especially of my mother's generation, Manhattan is Babylon on the Hudson, the kind of place where a young lady might fall victim to all manner of danger and ruin. My thinking was: Mama, if you have to ask, you'll never understand. New York has always been a magnet for misfit young Americans from small towns, who migrate there to find themselves, to test themselves, to be the selves they couldn't be back home.

My Birmingham girlfriend Becky understands. She'd come to know New York as a child herself, having traveled there several times with her musician mother. Still, Becky knows the mental blocks that separate Southerners of our generation from the idea of New York. "Sela, girl, I don't know how you found it within yourself to

move up there," Becky told me the other day. "When we were growing up, so many people had the idea that going to New York was
only slightly less scary than going to Russia."

I had to laugh, because she was right.

"Don't you remember? Our mother's friends thought it was the
kind of place where you could fall down dead of a heart attack
smack in the middle of Saks, and no one would do anything for
you," she said. "That there were so many people there, and nobody
was going to look out for you like they would back home, and how
you weren't going to make any friends?"

That's true, I told Becky, but I don't understand why our mothers—
our whole culture, really—raised us with such a distorted idea.

"You have to remember, honey, our side lost the Civil War. And
the South had a big ol' inferiority complex about the North that took
more than a hundred years to get over," Becky said. "But I think it
might be something deeper, too. You know how we are down here. If
I announced to all my friends that I was moving with my family from
Birmingham to Memphis, or Atlanta, or somewhere else down South,
by the end of the day I'd have a hundred names and phone numbers of
relatives, sorority sisters, and friends of my friends who live in the
new city. My Birmingham friends would call them up before we got
there, and they'd take us in like long-lost cousins, because that would
be the right thing to do. You and I know New York isn't as bad as most
older Southern folks think, but you have to admit you sure didn't find
anything like that when you went up there."

She's right, of course. When I left the South for Manhattan, it
was like going off the grid—that regional network of family and
friends that might have served me well as a safety net. But somehow,

at that moment in my life, I guess I'd had enough safety. The prospect of New York was intimidating, of course. But I don't remember ever doubting that I could make it there. I never stopped to think about how far I'd come. Where once I'd been too shy to confide in anyone but a mimosa tree, I was starting to become more surefooted, even outgoing; I suppose I was becoming a woman. Mama had no idea what to make of me, but just recently Daddy told me he saw a change that she might have missed. "Were you worried about me when I went off to New York?" I asked him.

"No," he said in his matter-of-fact way. "I worried when you went to Memphis, though."

So what was it that changed between Memphis and New York?

"Well, you'd been away from home some time. And I could see the difference. It just seemed like you knew how to meet people, get along on your own."

Did I have an easy time of it in New York? Did everything fall right into place? I don't think so—not at all. Nobody has an easy time of it when they first get to the big city. New York only seems easy to the young, whose idealism and lust for life cushions the heavy blows, and to the old and wealthy, whose money insulates them from the city's daily grind. But I was so in love with the city that the struggles I had there seem today only to have intensified what was for me an exhilarating experience. As Woody Allen once said, "It's not peaceful or easy, and because of it you feel more alive." Yes, absolutely, and if my memory has softened the hard edges of my New York years, it's because New York gave far more than it ever asked of me. It was the place where phantom dreams I only faintly knew I had began to come to life.

Of course, the friendships I'd made along the way also helped. Jim Lampley of ABC Sports and his girlfriend, Joanne, were so kind, taking me by the hand and weaving me into his network circles. Suddenly I found myself sitting at tables with Ivy League types, some of them reporters and producers from ABC News in Washington, up for the weekend. One of the men was dating a woman from the Kennedy clan. I didn't dare open my mouth for fear I'd say the wrong thing, or have nothing to say at all. Instead, I decided to keep my mouth shut and hoped I'd seem mysterious. I still remember the night I went over to Jim's apartment and heard John Coltrane and Thelonious Monk for the first time; I felt as if I'd entered some exotic new land, full of exciting sounds and challenges.

With all these new stimuli roiling around me, I have to admit I didn't spend a lot of time missing Meridian. I still called home every day, as always. But Mama was so protective of us kids, so desperate to make sure our lives turned out well, that she couldn't restrain herself from beckoning us home anytime she heard the slightest note of concern in my voice. Of course, it was wonderful to have that sense of security. But my mother could make the temptation seem overwhelming, and there were times when I just needed to resist the impulse to retreat into the womb of childhood. In those moments, it was my headstrong and fearless father's example I could always count on to guide me.

It wasn't homesickness that touched me in those days—it was a kind of wanderlust, a thirst for adventure. It was a feeling I'd first had on a trip to visit my cousins Judy and Tom Ward in Washington, D.C., after high school, years before. Judy took me to a bar in Georgetown, an old pub with lots of dark wood and brass fixtures: with its Old World clubby atmosphere, it reminded me of something out of *Brideshead Revisited*. It was there that I tasted a Bellini for the first time. Then I had dinner at Tom's apartment, and his girlfriend, Peggy, (now his wife) prepared fondue for dinner. Fondue! It seemed so *Continental*. As we sat around dipping our sirloin in the hot oil and our bread in the melted cheese, I remember just beaming like a little girl, inwardly at least. If a plain old pot of melted cheese (and, at long last, not of the Velveeta persuasion!) could turn me into a wide-eyed innocent abroad, a Henry James heroine swooning over the sensual richness of life in among the European swells, you can imagine how far I'd come.

And New York was the answer. For me it was like being a child getting to taste a new delicacy for the first time, every single day. One day I'd be having lunch at Café des Artistes, with an artist who lived in the same building; afterward I was invited up with friends to see his book-lined, painting-filled apartment—an outlander's perfect fantasy of a Manhattan aesthete's flat. The next day I'd find myself with other friends in the Upper East Side living room of the Halabys, the family of Jordan's Queen Noor, sneaking peeks at Her Majesty's family photographs. And here is the strangest thing: The feeling that draped over me in those early days in New York reminded me of nothing more than the joy I took from my childhood Christmases at Uncle Thomas's place, in that beautiful house, surrounded by the people I loved most. What could that possibly have to do with being all alone in a little apartment in a big Northern city? This: In both cases, I knew in my heart of hearts that I was standing exactly where I was supposed to be.

Which was enough to keep me happy—that is, until the rent came due. Remember, I was making only $6.50 an hour as a storyboard artist, and that wasn't enough to live on in the city, not even in the late seventies. Delta had rejected my flight-attendant application, saying they were afraid I couldn't be forceful enough for the job. (Back then, at least, they were probably right.) Eastern Airlines offered me a job, though, and I was planning to take it. I loved the idea of seeing the world, while always having a base in New York to come home to.

But then something else happened. A friend suggested that I try modeling, which certainly paid better than storyboarding—that is, if you got lucky and got hired. (After all, I wanted to eat at Le Cirque—at least once a year.) I'd tried it before: At the age of fifteen, following a young dream of mine, I'd gone to a local department store and entered a modeling contest held by a girls' clothing line. The winners would be flown to St. Louis and photographed for an ad in *Seventeen* magazine. I was one of the four winners from around the country, and off I went to Missouri, but that was as far as it went. Only when I got there did I discover that the ad was for bathing suits. Lord, I was so thin, and still had a boyish adolescent figure—the last thing they were looking for in a bathing-suit model. The creative director let all four of us know, in no uncertain terms, that not one of us had what it took to become a professional model. What a disaster.

But if at first you don't succeed . . . Jim Lampley was kind enough to offer to walk me around to some of the better modeling agencies, so I got all dressed up in my below-the-knee, pseudo-linen cream-colored skirt, a matching cream polyester blouse, and bone-colored heels, with my hair electric-rollered and ready. We got about two blocks before the heels came off, and I insisted on walking the rest of the way in my stocking feet. Jim was amused, but in a gentlemanly way; after all, he was from North Carolina.

Our first visit was to Eileen Ford's agency, where they got all excited and sent me to do a test shoot with a photographer. He sent me back with a Polaroid. Now, I ask you, who looks good in Polaroids? To some, I think, I looked like a Latina, but this was the era of Christie Brinkley and Cheryl Tiegs, the blond-haired, blue-eyed girl next door. Ms. Ford took one look at the Polaroid, and told the twenty-one-year-old white Anglo-Saxon Protestant standing in front of her, "Your look is too exotic. And your nose might be a bit of a problem." The next stop was Elite, where John Casablancas looked at *me* (instead of the Latina Polaroid), and said, "Your nose might be a bit of a problem."

My nose? I liked my nose. I'd never really thought about my nose. But I refused to take their word for it. I found out about a great fashion photographer, Hank Londoner, who'd got his start through the famous ex-model and modeling agent Wilhelmina. He agreed to shoot me, and the photos turned out spectacularly well, better than any I've had since. Wilhelmina looked at them, and even though she thought I was too short for my "exotic" look, bless her, she agreed to take me on.

As a child, I'd always been taught by my daddy to believe in myself. And I'd learned from my mother's example that the only way to get what you want is to keep at it. Now, with their wisdom running through my mind—and that New York spirit coursing through my veins—I'd finally proven that bathing-suit ad man in St. Louis wrong.

But I still had a lot to learn about New York. And one big eye-opener was right around the corner.

The first thing a professional model needs is a portfolio, a book of test shots to help potential clients see how you look on the page. So the agency sent me off to a photographer who, I'm told, had shot some big ads for high-end clothing lines. In hindsight he was probably a nobody, but I approached his studio as if he were an Avedon or a Scavullo. Big mistake.

This character's apartment was right down the hall from his studio, so I left my bag in his place and went down to the studio to begin shooting. As he was setting up the first shot, he turned to me, as casually as if he were commenting on the weather, and said, "You know, I'm celibate, and I have a chastity belt, and the key is in a safety deposit box."

"Oh, that's interesting," I said, wondering what kind of trouble I'd gotten myself into. *But I really need these pictures,* I told myself. *I can handle this.*

Then we started shooting . . . and he started snorting, line after line of cocaine, throughout the entire session. *Snap, snap, snort. Snap, snap, snort.* When we finished, as I was changing back into my street clothes, he headed back to his apartment, where I'd left my bag. And when I walked in to get it, there he was, lying spread-eagled on the floor, wearing nothing but a leather and metal contraption around his privates. He didn't say a word, but it was embarrassingly obvious that he was pretty happy to see me.

Without missing a beat, I stepped right over him and picked up my bag. Drawing on some hidden reserve of Southern-girl politesse, I said cheerily, "Well, thank you so much. It was very nice meeting you." When the elevator doors closed behind me, my knees nearly buckled.

Of course, this was the late 1970s, the peak of the disco era. Studio 54 was New York's center of gravity, and before long new clubs like Area were gaining on it. You'd go to the top clubs and find guys hanging out in the girls' bathroom, which at the time was a mark of sophistication. I loved the wildness of those places; even at the time I remember thinking, *Sela, you've never seen anything like this in your life.* And I was no homebody, believe me. I went out all the time, and saw it all. But when it came to debauchery I was always the observer, never really the participant.

Surveying the human wreckage of those times, especially the lives ruined and even lost due to drugs, I can only thank God I didn't go down that road. Part of me thinks I was saved because I never really ran in the same circles as most other models (I couldn't relate to them). But I remember being troubled by the spectacle of so many people giving their lives over to cocaine; it seemed plain to me that they were in a terrible rut, one I would do well to stay out of. And when things started swirling too fast around me, I thought of my father: thought of his strong will, of the way he never, but never, went with the crowd. He wasn't weak in that way, and his example may have saved my life.

The other Southern legacy that may have kept me sane was a little restaurant in Greenwich Village called the Pink Tea Cup. I'm not much of a cook; whenever I started longing for a little taste of home I'd call my Aunt Sarah or Aunt Nancy—the best cooks of our bunch—and ask them to walk me through one of their favorite recipes. But neither I nor my sister, Jenna, who moved to New York about a year after I did, could boil water without making a hash of it. So at least once a week we'd zip down to the Pink Tea Cup, a wonderful little soul-food joint owned and operated by Mary and Charles Raye, an African American couple from Florida. We'd eat fried pork chops, black-eyed peas, cornbread, turnip greens, and such for supper; if it was brunch we were after, Jenna would have homemade biscuits with maple syrup, and I'd order a big steaming bowl of grits. My sister and I would linger as long as we could there, enraptured by the flavors and aromas of our childhood.

The late Willie Morris was a Mississippian of Daddy's generation, who moved to New York in the late 1960s to be a magazine editor. In his memoir *North Toward Home*, Morris writes that people like us come from the country to New York not because we couldn't have succeeded back home, nor because we wanted to test ourselves. "We had always come, the most ambitious of us," he writes, "because we *had* to, because the ineluctable pull of the cultural capital when the wanderlust was high was too compelling to resist." He continues:

> Yet there were always secret dangers for these young people from the provinces in the city. It became

dangerously easy to turn one's back on his own past, on
the isolated places that nurtured and shaped him into
maturity, for the sake of some convenient or fashion-
able "sophistication." There were temptations to be not
merely careless, but dishonest, with the most distinc-
tive things about one's self. . . . Coming to New York
for the first time, the sensitive outlander might soon
find himself in a subtle interior struggle with himself,
over the most fundamental sense and meaning of his
own origins. It was this struggle, if fully compre-
hended, which finally could give New York its own
peculiar and wonderful value as a place, for it tested
who you are, in the deepest and most contorted way.

I can't say I ever felt quite the same intense internal conflict that tor-
mented Morris. I don't recall ever feeling ill at ease because I was
from the South, and I had an awful lot of fun in my years in New
York. But I do remember being ashamed of one thing about Mississippi, and that had to do with race. Like so many Southerners, I have
conflicted emotions about the place I love and call home, because its
ugly side is difficult to reconcile with my sweet memories.

When I was just eight years old, in 1964, Meridian became
ground zero in an explosion of violence and hatred that swept the
state after a group of young civil rights activists launched an effort
to register black voters. In the spring and summer of that year, the
Ku Klux Klan torched twenty black churches around the state,
Medgar Evers was shot and killed in Jackson, and three civil rights
activists based in Meridian were murdered by Klansmen.

Then, in June of that year, three civil rights workers—James Chaney, Andrew Goodman, and Michael Schwerner—were apprehended on a country road late at night, on their way to Meridian. Earlier that evening, while driving back from the site of a burned African American church in Neshoba County, they had been arrested by a local sheriff named Cecil Price. The sheriff released them at 10:00 P.M., but alerted local Klansmen to their whereabouts. Chaney, an African American from Meridian, and Goodman and Schwerner, Jews from New York, were killed brutally, their bodies removed from the scene; they would not be found for over a month. Authorities did find the bodies of *nine* other black men as they swept the nearby swamps and woods looking for the three. Nobody had ever bothered looking for those men before.

When they finally found the bodies of Chaney, Goodman, and Schwerner, the corpses were stacked on top of one another in an earthen dam. The headline in the *Meridian Star* the next day: THE NIGGER WAS FOUND ON TOP. The parents of the three dead young men attempted to have them buried together in the same Meridian cemetery, but were prevented from doing so because local laws extended segregation even to the graveyard.

This incident, which occurred roughly an hour's drive from my home, became the subject of a landmark trial in which nineteen conspirators were indicted and seven convicted; two decades later it was the basis of the film *Mississippi Burning*.

These terrible events were barely a decade behind us when I came to New York. I knew that, as a white person from Mississippi, I would be considered by many of those I met as a product, a *member*, of the culture that killed those men and so many others throughout the South, from the time of slavery through the civil rights era. I despised the racism and brutality that had gone on in my state, and I shuddered to think of myself as bearing any association with it.

As a Southerner, as a Meridian native, I *was*, of course, associated with it—if only by the accident of my hometown. But at the same time, that vile racism was never a part of my direct experience in childhood—it could not be found, that is, in the hearts of the people immediately around me. My parents completely sheltered us from the degradation and terror whites inflicted upon blacks in those days, and our home was not tainted by the venomous racism endemic to our society. Of course I now see that we lived in an all-white neighborhood, and the blacks lived on the other, poorer side of town. It sounds impossible to believe now, but in those days it was possible not to see what you didn't want to see—or, to be more precise, what others didn't want you to see. The terrible human toll Jim Crow took on black Americans was something I lived through as a child, but only became fully aware of as an adult.

The wickedness of segregation was so great, and its wounds so long-lasting, that it's still hard to credit the brotherhood that really did exist between many blacks and whites then. But it did happen. It was only years later that I learned how some white families, including my own, had all along been quietly helping change things for the better—and risking their lives to do it. My Uncle Thomas, for example, and his friend Al Rosenbaum were intimately involved in leading the white resistance to the Ku Klux Klan.

"In the summer of '68, the synagogue in town had been bombed, and we knew the Klan was beginning to launch a reign of terror," Al remembers. "Tom and I were part of a big group called the Committee of Conscience, which met at the Episcopal church once a month. We brought in ministers from other white churches, and some of their people, as well as black leaders. Our purpose was to say, We've got to educate our children, and we've got to do the best we can to get along under integration.

"We put up the money through this Committee of Conscience, and helped the FBI infiltrate the KKK group, and found out when they were going to come next and what they were going to do," Al continues. "We found out the Klan was planning to kill a Meridian businessman named Meyer Davidson, who was a leader in the community. There was a shootout on a Saturday night between the Klan on one side, and the FBI and the Meridian police on the other. The woman who was the driver for the Klan leader was killed, and the leader was badly mangled. He went to jail."

Nine years after the bloody shootout, which was sparked by a KKK plot to assassinate a Jewish leader, Meridian elected its first Jewish mayor: Al Rosenbaum. "That was unbelievable," Al reflects now, and he's right: Mississippi's seemingly intractable legacy of injustice is finally, permanently, becoming part of the past.

My friend Clifton Taulbert is one of the wisest men I know on this subject. Cliff, who is black, grew up in segregated Glen Allan, Mississippi, and his memories of growing up in the Delta form the basis of his extraordinary memoir *Once Upon a Time When We Were Colored*. I have learned a lot from *Eight Habits of the Heart*, a short inspirational volume Cliff wrote several years ago. In it he tells stories about the kindness of a Jewish family to him as a child, allowing him to break the social code and come into their kitchen to eat lunch. He tells of a white doctor and her black nurse who worked together to heal sick people of both races, and how two female educators, each of whom oversaw the segregated schools of her own race, worked together for the benefit of all students, in gentle defiance of the prevailing social attitudes.

"Brotherhood is such a powerful habit of the heart that even when only one person reaches out to do right, the impact can be lifelong," Cliff writes. "If I had not encountered this habit of the heart when I was young, I could have left the South embittered and hurt. Instead I left with purpose and a plan. I could not have done so without the memory of these acts of brotherhood. I needed to see them practiced in front of me to believe that they could happen."

He who binds himself to a joy
Does the winged life destroy;
But he who kisses the joy as it flies
Lives in eternity's sunrise.

—WILLIAM BLAKE

With Jenna in New York City.

4 ◢)

....

"Dowwn-towwn," my teacher said.

"Daywn-taywn," I repeated.

"Dowwn-towwn."

"Daywn-taywn."

We went on like this for hours. "Every time you pronounce the word that way," Henry said, "you must get a toothache."

My teacher was Henry Jacoby, a legendary voice coach who lived on West End Avenue in a massive, shadowy prewar building. And in those early days I spent in New York, I passed many an afternoon there with Henry, trying desperately to flatten out one of my most obvious hometown holdovers—my Southern drawl. I had to, for I was going to become an actress.

Much to my delighted surprise, my modeling career had taken off more quickly than I'd dared to hope. My break came when the Screen Actors Guild went on strike. A friend of a friend worked at an ad agency that was desperate to find an actress for a Maybelline cosmetics TV spot. They hired me for the princely sum of $100 an hour. I couldn't believe my good fortune. It seemed as if, after years of floating down a lazy river, I'd suddenly hit the rapids.

But when the TV commercial division of Wilhelmina started sending me out on more auditions, I ran smack into my first professional challenge: I didn't know how to act. I was fine one-on-one with the camera, but as soon as I had to exchange dialogue with another actor I'd freeze up. Time to start taking some acting classes, I thought. Learn the craft. Lose the drawl.

Henry, God bless him, was probably eighty years old when he took me on as a student. His building was close to Lincoln Center; on the elevator ride up to his flat, you'd inevitably hear pianists practicing in their apartments, and opera singers working out the kinks in their arias. I was still wide-eyed enough that walking the halls of Henry's building made me feel I was taking a leap down some Gotham rabbit hole.

Henry was so ancient, and his flowing white hair made him appear to be an angel. He was the kind of aristocratic character you move to the big city to meet. Whenever the phone would ring in the middle of a lesson, he would raise his bony finger like a wizard's wand, and say mischievously, "Saved by the bell." During our lessons Henry would strike notes on the piano, and teach me to sound them out in response. He had a copy of Kahlil Gibran's *The Prophet* close at hand, and at the end of every lesson he would open it and

HEIGHT 5'7½"
DRESS 6-7-8
BUST 34
WAIST 24
HIPS 34
SHOE 8B

GLOVE 6½
HAT 21½
HAIR Brunette
EYES Hazel
S.A.G.
EXCELLENT HANDS

Wilhelmina

9 EAST 37 STREET
NEW YORK CITY
PRINT: 532-6800
TV: 889-9450
FASH. SHOWS 686-2454

Wilhelmina West

inc./TALENT AGENTS

(213) 553 9525

My first modeling card.

ask me to recite a passage. As someone whose accent marinated in the Mississippi mud, I had the hardest time with words like "downtown," those diphthongs coming out like two long flat notes played on a trumpet.

It turned out I had a good ear for accents, though, and with a little hard work it wasn't long before I'd conquered my drawl. I worked a lot on the quality of my voice, to make it less nasal and more throaty. Plus, it helped that I wasn't hanging out with a bunch of Southerners, tempting my ear to fall back into my old familiar cadences.

But good pronunciation wasn't going to save my acting career.

So I started studying with a teacher named Bob McAndrew. It was one of those life-changing decisions. Under Bob's guidance I began a transformation from quiet, introspective, small-town girl to confident woman who was unafraid to take big risks on the public stage. More important, for the first time I began to see, and to believe, that there was something more to me than a pretty face.

I continued modeling to pay the bills, but discovered that acting was my true passion; it held out a promise of personal fulfillment that modeling could not. Being judged simply on your looks twenty times a day is a rotten way to earn a living—for me, at least—and it's bound to turn you into a neurotic mess. For every person who flipped through my portfolio and thought my look was great, there were ten others who'd hand it back with a curt "Thank you" and escort me out the door. I relentlessly pounded the pavements of lower Manhattan, where many of the top fashion photography studios were, repeatedly submitting myself to this cattle-call rating of my appearance. At times it felt like a nonstop parade of rejection, but soon enough I started encountering a little acceptance, too— enough that I was finally able to quit asking Mama for money, and to live pretty well as a twenty-two-year-old.

But it was a dehumanizing kind of work, and I knew I wouldn't be able to take it for long. Acting class was where my heart was. Bob McAndrew taught at an acting school in the theater district on the West Side. The owner was a well-known acting coach, but if you had no experience you went to Bob's class. We first met in a small theater within the American Place Theatre building on West Forty-sixth Street. The students sat looking down from the audience onto the tiny stage, where we'd do endless exercises, and lots of listening.

Corbin Bernsen was in my class; years later we'd work together again, on *L.A. Law* and the movie *Hello Again,* and it was like a little two-person class reunion. We were all nobodies then, but being in a New York acting class seemed at the time to be the most meaningful thing I could possibly do with my life.

Bob left to start his own acting studio in the Forties between Eighth and Ninth Avenues, and we followed him. It was like a little club. Our group spent almost a year together in this class, young, eager, and intoxicated by hope and possibility. We produced plays to showcase our acting chops for agents; everybody would pitch in and help with scenery and sets. After our performances we'd all go out for beers and talk late into the night about what we were going to do with our lives once we got our big break. I was coming out of myself, learning how to enjoy life.

Having completed my acting classes and polished up my fresh new north-of-nowhere accent, I was ecstatic when my agent called to say she'd landed me a two-day role on *One Life to Live:* Nurse Bunny Cahill. The name alone should have told me something about the nature of the role. Nurse Bunny was in love with a doctor, and almost every line she uttered had to do with offering him food: "Would you like some Chinese food, Doctor?" "I'm having apple pie á la mode—would you like to join me, Doctor?" (Years later David Letterman would have some fun with this, stringing all of Nurse Bunny's little one-liners together: the accumulated screen time couldn't have added up to more than two and a half minutes.) We weren't talking Tennessee Williams here.

Call me naive, but I was startled to see what an assembly line soap-opera production was. The director was invisible, hidden off in a booth somewhere, and the whole process churned along like a machine—efficient, businesslike, but sterile, and not at all what I'd been looking forward to after all those good creative sessions with Bob McAndrew. There was none of the spontaneous creativity, none of the camaraderie—not to mention, of course, none of the great material. Before too long I was offered a regular role on another day-time soap; I was flattered that the producers liked me enough to ask me, but if this was what acting was, I just didn't want any part of it. Big break or not, I turned it down.

I'd reached a crossroads. Something inside was telling me I might have what it took to make it as an actress. But with precious few acting jobs on the New York stage, and little TV and movie production in New York at the time, what choice did I have?

I thought: Sela, if you can make it here, you can sure as hell make it in Los Angeles. New York had put me to the test, and gave me a hint about what I might really have been meant to do with my life. I had no idea where my destiny was going to take me, but I knew beyond a doubt that it wasn't back home to Mississippi. New York had shown me that. But I'd done all I thought I could do there. If acting really was my calling, I convinced myself, there was only one way to find out for sure: pull up my still-forming New York roots, go to Hollywood, and roll the dice.

I packed up my things and bought a one-way ticket to L.A.

That January day in 1983, I stepped off the plane at LAX with nothing but what I could carry in a suitcase, the name of an agent,

With Jenna (far left), Mama (far right), and friends in New York.

and a promise from a friend that a Hollywood buddy of his would meet me at the airport. Where I got the courage to trust this stranger to pick me up and deliver me safely to a hotel, I'll never know. It just seemed like a chance worth taking.

And I got lucky: The stranger turned out to be a sweetheart. He drove me straight to the Beverly Hills Hotel, the pink stucco palace on Sunset Boulevard, where we met his sister in the famous Polo Lounge for lunch. They invited me to a party that night at one of the hotel bungalows to watch the miniseries *The Winds of War*. I met a guy there named Mark, who was the assistant to a studio big, and he invited me to join him and his friends the next day for brunch. And so I did. Within twenty-four hours of arriving in Los Angeles, I had a network of interesting new friends. It was a lovely introduction to my new city.

This was so different from my experience in New York, where people tended to be insular and defensive, and you felt as if you had to fight for everything. Was everything in L.A. going to be this easy? Surely not, but I had reason to hope.

I stayed at the Beverly Hilton for two weeks, and by the end of that time I'd landed my first movie role: through a friend of a friend, I was cast for a part in *The Man Who Loved Women*, a Burt Reynolds movie. What a moment! Burt was at the peak of his career at that point. To make sure I could handle the part—which wasn't much more than a single scene—the director, Blake Edwards, sent me to an acting coach: Nina Foch, who'd been nominated for an Oscar for her role in *Executive Suite* in 1954. It was magical: There I was sitting at her house up in one of the canyons, the two of us being served tea by her Asian butler as she instructed me on the role and steered me toward classes I should take. The sun-drenched languor of Los Angeles was a world away from the harried, gray intensity of Manhattan, but I loved it in the same way. Once again I seemed to have floated into a heady new landscape worlds away from what I'd left behind.

I don't mean to give the impression that trying to make it as an actress in L.A. was easy. It's just that I had lived for years in New York, where everything is a struggle. L.A. seemed to have no hard edges, at least none that this hardened Manhattanite felt at the time. I did have to return to modeling, though, to sustain my new life.

One of our infamous L.A. dinner parties.

One of the first things I did when I arrived in town was to check in with the Wilhelmina office. When I wasn't trying to get acting roles, I took modeling jobs—often catalogue work, which is the dinner theater of the modeling world—to pay the rent on the tiny West Hollywood studio apartment into which I'd moved. I didn't want to model, and I certainly didn't want to do it for catalogues, but whatever it took to keep my Hollywood dreams alive, I was willing to do. At the time I still believed that the Hollywood Walk of Fame was the road to happiness.

Things moved quickly for me. Five months after relocating I found myself at the Cannes Film Festival, at the Hotel du Cap-Eden Roc with a friend who was promoting a movie. We were dining at

the hotel's famed restaurant overlooking the Mediterranean, drinking $200 bottles of white burgundy with dinner. It was the most delicious wine I'd ever tasted. Suddenly, the timid girl from Meridian who used to tell secrets to the mimosa tree had plopped herself right in the middle of a jet-setty Hollywood life. Being footloose on the French Riviera is a long way from walking barefoot on the Mississippi Gulf Coast—and I was loving every minute of it.

But it wasn't as if I'd severed all my connections with the past. For months I actually hung on to my New York apartment, flying back as often as I could to see my friends and reconnect with that city I hadn't yet had my fill of. And from time to time I came back to Meridian, too, to recharge my batteries and crawl back into the womb. Even when I was just starting out in New York, when I had to eat day-old bagels to make sure I had enough cash to get me

Being held by Grandma while Aunt Sara,
Daddy's sister, feeds me.

With my summer parasol.

We Wards: from left to right, Brock, Berry, Jenna, me.

Being named a Phi Kappa Little Sister.

Studying and dreaming: in my bedroom during high school.

With my sorority sister Ann Hale.

With Daddy on the porch swing.

From *Southeastern Conference Football* magazine, 1977.

Honey Watching
On a Saturday Afternoon

"You gulls, you only come t' see me because you wanna get yo' picture taken": with Coach Bear Bryant.

In my Wilhelmina
modeling days.

In Rome on our first trip to Europe:
(left to right) Brock, Jenna, Berry, and me.

The happiest day of my life: dancing with Howard at my wedding.

With the cast of *Sisters*.

With Harrison Ford, my leading man in *The Fugitive*.   Winning the Emmy for *Once & Again* in 20

With my *Once & Again* costar, Billy Campbell.

On the porch at the
Rose Cottage: Anabella...

. . . and Austin with their Easter Bunny gifts.

I've always had a porch
swing, and I always will.

With Mama in 1994
(I was pregnant with Austin at the time).

On the porch of the
log cabin playhouse.

through the week, I had always managed to put away enough savings to get home when I needed to. You can always find a way to get home to your mama.

Whenever I hear people mention casually that they haven't been home to see their families in years, it's as if they're speaking another language. I still remember once, after breaking off one of my relationships, how eager I was to get back with Mama, to have the time to talk with her and have her listening ear; to have her make my favorite yellow cake with milk-chocolate icing and pecans on top, and let me know all was right with the world. What else is home for, if not comfort and consolation?

But I was starting to think about making a home in L.A., too. I'd been eyeing a historic West Hollywood building called La Fontaine, and when a flat came available that had been styled by Waldo Fernandez, a famous L.A. decorator, I jumped at it. It was chic and contemporary, like living in a sophisticated dream. The owner of the building, Alfredo de la Vega, lived next door; he was kind and paternal and endlessly gracious, always eager to look after me and offer help when I needed it.

Here in L.A. it was easier to come by like-minded young actors than in New York; my part of town was home to a lot of up-and-coming artists, writers, and other creative types, and before long my little crew of friends had become a genuine social circle, my building its own little village.

There was plenty of free time between auditions, so my friends and I had lots of opportunities for entertaining. We began throwing theme parties. One night I had a black-tie dinner party à la Noël Coward; we all dressed up and sat around the table reading one of his one-act plays aloud, and by the end of the evening I had a living

room full of elegant couples dancing on chairs I'd borrowed from Alfredo's basement. And one summer afternoon we had a Renoir picnic in the backyard. I'd always loved his painting *The Luncheon of the Boating Party*, a portrait of a nineteenth-century outdoor feast on a floating barge—a motley collection of marvelous people, thrown together for an afternoon's enjoyment. So that day we became the Boating Party, or as close as we could manage, flowered hats and all, and drank wine and laughed as I practiced talking in my "new voice."

One weekend, of course, the dream, like all good dreams, had to come to an end. While I was away on location in San Francisco, my landlord, Alfredo, was murdered. When I heard what had happened, I thought immediately: *The killer had walked right by my door.*

I took Alfredo's death hard; he'd always been so kind to me. I kept thinking back to a big dinner party I'd been preparing not long before, and of that sweet man offering to lend me some dishes. "Oh, just keep them when you're done." Being a proper Southern woman, of course, I said, "No, no, I couldn't possibly"—and gave them back. After he died, I regretted it terribly. If I had only been gracious enough to accept Alfredo's gift, I would have had something to remember him by.

In 1983 my agent, Steve Dontanville—who believed in me when I was a nobody, and still does, which is why he's still my agent all these years later—got me an audition for a role on a new TV series, a drama called *Emerald Point N.A.S.* He gave me a few pages of the audition script sent over by the casting agent. But when I arrived at the audition, they gave me ten *new* pages to read—a part of the script I'd never seen.

Being too young and foolish to know any better, I figured I could pull it off. We'd done many cold readings back in Bob McAndrew's classes. I asked for a few minutes to look over my lines, and then came out and sat before a stone-faced female casting agent and her assistant in the front row, with several of the show's producers behind them. I started to read, but when I heard the panic in my own voice I stopped and asked if I could start over. The casting agent rolled her eyes, then snickered toward her assistant. I waited an eternity before she cast a baleful eye at me then recited the opening line, my signal to start over. Which I did. But her rudeness had shaken me, and my reading was dreadful. To no

As Hilary Adams on Emerald Point N.A.S.

one's surprise, the role—a femme fatale named Hilary Adams—went to someone else.

I ran out of that audition into a driving rain, found a phone booth, called a friend, sobbed about hating Hollywood and how much I wanted to move back to New York. But then the unexpected happened. When they started shooting the *Emerald Point* pilot, the actress they'd chosen to play Hilary bombed. The producers called me back, this time to read for a different casting agent—and this time I got the part.

The show lasted only one season, but it gave me my first major acting work, and while I was shooting it I met my first serious L.A. boyfriend, an actor. He had a place way up in Topanga Canyon, an Australian shepherd named Whisky, and a way of adding a sense of romantic adventure to everything we did.

Naturally, I took my beau home to meet my family. Everybody got along well, but this was the first time I'd been back home since getting my steady job on television, and to be honest it made the trip a little different. The kindest folks—family, close friends—were proud of me; I could have been eking out a living doing Ty-D-Bowl commercials and my folks would have been supportive—but of course there were others who were, well, more *reserved* in their congratulations. And then there were the people who couldn't seem to separate me from what I was doing on-screen—a problem that's dogged me ever since. Years later, when I was on *Sisters*, they'd come up to me and say, "I can't believe you painted the word 'slut' on your sister's new Porsche!" I'd smile and cock my head and try to explain to them that that wasn't really me, but something in them couldn't separate the two.

My actor boyfriend and I were together for about three years. I was crazy about him—so much so that I began to put my career on hold so I could travel with him. In truth, I can't help feeling now that my small-town upbringing hampered my judgment—because I was convinced, I realize now, that I couldn't be more successful than the man I was with. And while this man was a romantic figure, he was also something of a cipher—elusive, unavailable, at times passive-aggressive. Things began to sour between us when he went up to do some location work in Vancouver. I moved up there to be with him, to have the romantic experience of taking in a new city together. But after only a week he freaked out, complaining that he needed his space. I packed my bags and called a car to take me to the airport; on the way there I got the driver to give me a quick tour of the city—the tour I never got with my boyfriend.

I really thought the two of us would one day be married, but he was terrified of that kind of thing. I should have seen it coming, but it was only when we were thrown into such proximity that I saw just how afraid of commitment he really was. And I think it was also in that moment that I first began to realize how much the idea of having a family meant to me.

But knowing what you want and having the willpower to choose it don't always go hand in hand. After this first Hollywood relationship, I became involved with another actor. (You'd think I would have learned my lesson!) Again, we were together for just over three years; again we had good times together. But once again I knew in my heart I shouldn't give myself over to the wrong man—this one a tough, domineering figure who was still in search of himself. As much as I had accomplished on my own, I was still struggling with the emotional conflicts that come with Southern womanhood. It was hard to resist deferring to the will of strong men, no matter how unhappy that made me. Lingering memories of my upbringing told me that was the way things were supposed to be, even though I knew better. I got to the point where I was turning down roles, and was prepared to sacrifice my career if the man I loved demanded it.

What finally made me leave that relationship was the simple realization that he wasn't cut out to be a husband and a father—not the husband I wanted to have kids with, anyway. Marriage? Children? Yes. Mark it down to boredom, the biological clock, or (as I believe) maturity, but I was in my early thirties, and the glittery novelty of the Hollywood life was starting to fade.

A big part of it, I'm sure, was that I was beginning to miss the friendships I had with women back home. Women like Jeanne Fort, whom I'd known since ninth grade, or my sorority suitemates from college, Ginger Drago, Connie Crutchfield, and Ann Hale. Women who'd been there to share stories, and laughter, and dreams—but who now were hundreds of miles away, and already started on families of their own.

It's not that I lacked for female friends in L.A.; it's that women in an aggressive, industry-driven culture like Hollywood often aren't friends with each other in quite the same way.

For one thing, it's hard for women who are in show business to be friends. Too often you're competing for the same roles, which doesn't always make for easy honesty in your relationships. I was once close to a well-known actor and his actress girlfriend, who is my age. After they married, though, his career took off like a rocket, and she eventually dropped me; it was the first time I really felt the sting of the unforgiving Hollywood food chain, and the distrust it can foster. Women can be each other's worst enemies when they think their survival's at stake (a lesson I should have learned back in high school Hell Week).

There's just no substitute for the sublime pleasures of Southern girltalk. Pining away one rainy weekend in Meridian last year, I phoned my friends Becky and Liz and invited them over from Birmingham for a visit. We sat around the kitchen table at my sister-in-law Hallie's place, and with the kids all upstairs playing, we opened a couple of bottles of red wine, kicked back, and started gabbing. When I walked in with the cheese and crackers, Becky was holding forth on the subject of marital discretion.

"Like I was saying, Sela, of course a woman's got to be passionate with her husband. But at the same time, it would be totally inappropriate to sit down at the country club and talk about the private, intimate things that happen between you and your husband. You just don't respect women who do that."

"Well," said Liz, "in my sewing group, people say things."

"Your sewing group?" I said. "You sew?"

"Honey, nobody sews," Liz replied. "We just talk."

"That's how my bunco group was," said Hallie. (Bunco is a dice game Southern women adore.) "I was in it for eight years, but I finally decided I wasn't going to sit around and talk about women who had breast implants when I was going to be one of 'em."

Everybody hooted, and started telling stories about their adventures in cosmetic surgery. Becky barreled into an epic account of her post-childbirth liposuction "to take care of that little roll that just would not go away."

"So I went into that doctor's office in this hospital, and I was sitting in this cute little Louis XIV chair, and it was so lovely. Honey, I was going in style. It just felt good to be there," Becky said.

"Then when I went in for surgery, it was this awful fluorescent light, and it was stark, and oooooh, you just don't look good. No makeup, no nail polish, no anything. Just like God sent you into this world. Any wrong thing you've ever eaten in your life is there under bright lights for all the world to see."

Becky took a big swallow of her wine, then started describing how the doctor—whom she knew socially—made marks on her abdomen to guide him in the surgery.

"I was just so mortified!" Becky said. "No makeup on! Buck-naked, with this man who is my neighbor, who I go to Christmas parties with, just marking up my body in front of my husband, who was there, and this good-looking intern, the nurse, and the scrub. Oh, it was horrid, and they were just jolly about it all. They got me up on the table and asked me what they could do for me, and I told them just to call Dr. Kevorkian because I can *take no more*."

The rest of us were laughing so hard we nearly fell out of our chairs. When we caught our breath, Becky reassured us that the surgery had actually gone well, with few side effects—except for those stubborn markings. "I had a big old '86' on my left butt-cheek, all in black marker, for about a month," Becky said.

"You know, I was open about my lipo with all my friends. But it put them in a real dilemma. Wouldn't it be bad form to run a casserole over to somebody who just got out of the hospital for liposuction?"

"Oh, all my friends have had breast implants," said Hallie, "and everybody's running casseroles over to their houses when they come home from the hospital."

"But don't you see, when you have breast implants, you're putting something on, so that's okay," Becky said. "With lipo, you're taking something off. Running a casserole over is like taking a pack of Marlboros over to a smoker who just had a lung removed."

We had some more wine, and talked about makeup, and our mamas, and our childhoods, and all the things that I rarely get to talk about so intimately in L.A. At one point the conversation turned to friends we know who have suffered from breast cancer, which prompted Liz to tell a story that, for me, represents what being a woman in the South is all about.

"Our friend Beth"—not her real name—"had finished her chemo, and she was getting ready to go into the hospital to have her breast removed," Liz began. "She was supposed to go in at eleven, so at eight o'clock that morning, her best girlfriends all went over to her house and piled up in the bed with her, and we cried and laughed and just talked about fun times that we'd had.

"Her husband was there, and he was kind of staying away, just letting us girls be girls. There was one girl who had also suffered through breast cancer, and she had had breast removal and reconstruction surgery. Poor Beth was just so scared, but this girl showed Beth her breast, to let her know that it was nothing to be afraid of, to give her the strength to face it.

"She showed Beth that, and Beth asked, 'Would you mind showing my husband, so he won't be scared, too?' And she did. There was hardly a dry eye in the room. There was nothing bad about it at all. In fact, I'd say it was the kindest thing I've ever seen."

Everybody around the table was quiet. Then Becky jumped in.

"During Beth's illness, Liz more than once called me and said, 'I'm a mess. I just left Beth's bedside. Where are you?' And more than once she came over and cried her eyes out. She had a broken heart. I sat there with tissues, holding her and putting her back together.

"And one time, Cornelius, our yard man, whose mother and sister died of breast cancer, saw what was going on, and he came inside and prayed with us for our friend," Becky continued. "He had big ol' tears running down his cheeks. I adore that man. The next day he came by with a cassette tape of a healing sermon his pastor had preached—preached!—just for Beth. And you know, as soon as Beth was feeling better, she wrote him a note. Now, that's a Southern woman for you!"

That image—of the friends and neighbors who helped Beth in her fight for life—stayed on my mind long after that weekend. It brought back so much about what I missed about small-town life, and about the emotional solidarity Southern women have with each other, especially in times of adversity. It reminded me of the power of faith in God, of its power to heal and to cement bonds between people linked as closely as those women, or as tenuously as an ailing woman and her friend's considerate gardener.

By comparison to the lives Becky and Liz live in Birmingham, women can really be considerably more isolated from each other in the bigger coastal cities, especially if they have no family around, or no strong history with the women around them. There are very few women in my life with whom I would be close enough to comfort them tenderly on a morning before surgery. We could never be as demonstrative. We'd be more concerned about respecting each other's space and privacy than we would about offering a hand in consolation.

Those women who climbed into bed with Beth have a closeness born of years spent together, and of shared history. Taking the time to foster that kind of relationship is something I really miss. In my Hollywood life, I know that even the best people I know spend so much of their time in their own heads, worrying over their own problems—myself among them. It's just too difficult to be giving in that atmosphere, to think as often as we should of others. Instead we lead quiet inner lives, behind invisible shields that close us off from most true intimacy.

This is especially true in Hollywood because it's such an ego-driven company town. Most of the people I know are in show business, so work is an understood part of every conversation. Social relationships are often corrupted by the suspicion, valid or not, that somebody is befriending you only because of what they think you can do for them. Once, when I was up-and-coming, I ran into an actress from a popular 1980s primetime soap. I found a moment to tell her how much I admired her work. It wasn't false flattery; I just wanted to give her something by acknowledging how much she'd given me through her work.

"Oh, thank you, that's nice," she said curtly, then turned around and went about her business. I was crushed. How can you hope to build lasting friendships in a town where warm words are met only by a cold shoulder?

I don't pretend it'll always be easy for me to build that kind of bond—the kind that comes with uninterrupted years spent breathing the same air—during the time I spend in Meridian. And yet I've found I can come back home and fall into fast friendships with women I haven't known since childhood. Southerners know this well: when you meet a Southerner in another part of the world—whether in New York, California, or overseas—you can't stop talking to each other. A lot of natural barriers between strangers collapse at once. You speak the same language, share so much common culture. I didn't get to know my dear friend Manny Mitchell, a Meridian native, and his terrific wife, Melanie, until we started working on a project together recently, but Manny was no stranger to me. He's been part of my life all that time. And expatriated Southerners are almost always living among people more reserved than they, so they fall all over themselves with excitement at the chance to swap stories with a sympathetic soul.

My boyfriend and I broke up right before I got the role of Teddy Reed on *Sisters,* and about then something in me snapped. As I say, I was getting tired of subjugating my own dreams to the whims of ill-suited men; what I needed was a new outlook.

I had always had long, silky hair, in the classic Southern mold, and I was reluctant to cut it during my modeling career because I was getting TV commercials and print ads for hair-care products. My whole look was that of the well-put-together, modern Southern belle—which might have had something to do with why I kept getting offered ice-princess roles. Well, it was time for a change. My looks didn't honestly reflect who I'd become—much more of a risk-taker, much less reliant on my physical appearance, and more confident about my ability as an actor. So I had my locks chopped short, put away my vast collection of cream-colored silk blouses and skirts, and started wearing T-shirts and jeans. For the first time in my life I felt free from my looks—ready to offer more than what you see on an eight-by-ten glossy.

That one simple gesture really changed the way I felt. Maybe it would take a psychologist to explain why. All I know is, suddenly I felt more free to express myself—as if I'd finally lifted some more profound weight off my shoulders. I started to have more fun. I was happier.

And I'm sure it also had to do with my work on *Sisters*. Teddy Reed was unlike any character I'd ever played. The producers had wanted me for yet another ice-princess role—the corporate, career-driven sister, who ended up being played by Julianne Phillips. But I was so tired of those parts; they made me feel as if I were choking. I took a chance and showed up for the audition in jeans, a tank top, and a black leather jacket, hair cropped short, ready for a risk. And, thank God, I got the part.

Teddy Reed was the role that would make a real actress out of me. It was like going to acting class on a daily basis, week after week. I studied very hard with my brilliant coach, Shawn Nelson, on every script over the entire six years. The role was an enormous challenge, one that forced me to stretch in every direction. Teddy was an alcoholic, which was painful for her, but which allowed me to explore a range of stormy emotions on camera. Once I had to play Teddy as blasted at her sister's wedding, shooting up the crystal with a shotgun. In another episode, Teddy tenderly comforted a friend dying of AIDS; in another, the script called for Teddy to play farce. Sometimes, I'd pick up the next episode's script, terrified of what they wanted Teddy to do, praying I'd find a way to pull it off. And sometimes, frankly, I felt as if I'd fallen flat on my face—though it seemed as though the next episode always offered a chance to redeem myself.

Learning to play that volatile character freed me to be more confident and expressive in my personal life. Because there was comedy in almost every *Sisters* script, I started to find more humor and fun in the world around me. At long last, years after I left the South to chase my dream, I was becoming the woman I'd always hoped to be. By the time *Sisters* ended its six-year run I'd been given an Emmy for my acting—but my real reward was this new, stronger sense of myself.

And part of that transformation was knowing a little more about what I wanted in my personal life. I'd finally matured to the point of knowing I didn't need a man to be happy. But I knew now, just as powerfully, that what I *wanted* was a husband and children. Just as I couldn't be fully myself without my career, I knew my life would be incomplete without a soul mate to marry, and, in time, children to nurture and love. I was tired of living in a house. I wanted a home.

Of course, as Flannery O'Connor said, a good man is hard to find—and she'd never even been to Hollywood. I'd had it with self-involved actors, whose egos were so insatiable and fragile that they couldn't make room for anyone else in their lives—never mind committing to lifelong marriage or fatherhood.

One day in 1991, during the first season of *Sisters*, a friend of mine said she knew a businessman, a private investor, who seemed perfect for me. She wanted to introduce us. I thought, *Why not? If he doesn't work in show business, he stands a chance of being a sane, normal person.* I agreed to meet him on a blind date.

Come live with me, and be my love,
And we will all the pleasures prove
That valleys, groves, hills and fields,
Woods, or steepy mountain yields.

—Christopher Marlowe

5 ❧

Howard was as blasé about meeting me as I was about meeting him. When our mutual friend, Carrie, the matchmaker, called to tell him about me, he was curious . . . until she told him what I did for a living.

"She's an actress," Carrie said.

"Wait, stop right there. Completely not interested," Howard told her. He'd grown up in Los Angeles; he knew actresses were a dime a dozen.

"Well, she's a *working* actress," she said.

"Even worse," Howard replied. "Let me tell you what she probably is: an actress who's dated lots of actors, and she wants to meet a regular guy."

"Yes, that's right."

"Here's the thing," Howard explained. "We regular guys, we put our pants on one leg at a time. We're mortals. We're not going to call and say, 'The jet will pick you up and we're meeting Woody Allen for lunch in Barbados.' When you're dating actors, it's a whole different world. She probably thinks she wants a regular guy, but she'll think it's not exciting enough."

Carrie tried for three weeks to sell Howard on the idea of a date with me. Finally she told him, "Howard, I don't think you understand. I've only set up three couples on a blind date in my life, and all three couples ended up getting married."

Based on that track record, the man who would become my husband agreed to meet me.

But first he decided to do a little research of his own. He rented *Nothing in Common*, a film I'd been in with Tom Hanks, to see what I was like on-screen. My character in that movie was one of those ice princesses I'd been trying to get away from before I got *Sisters*, but it was the only time he'd ever seen me. So he became convinced that in real life I was just like my character—"Kind of a typical L.A. woman, been-there-done-that, nothing impresses them," he says today. Carrie told him I was a football fan, so he suggested the four of us—Carrie and her boyfriend, Howard and I—take in a Raiders game, for what he was sure would be our one and only date.

Carrie arranged for the three of us to meet Howard on a street corner and drive to the stadium together. He was late, and when he finally arrived he pulled up in his car and said, "Follow me." Follow him? Sure, he was tall and handsome, but was this guy raised by wolves? We three tailed him in Carrie's car, and when we stopped at a red light I got out of Carrie's car, walked up to his window, and said, "Shouldn't I be sitting in this car?"

In the thirty minutes it took us to drive to the stadium, though, my impression of Howard Sherman began to change. Dressed in jeans and a faded green turtleneck, he seemed so comfortable, quietly sure of himself. There was no posturing, no trying too hard, and he wasn't wrapped up in himself. And in his presence, somehow, I just felt safe.

We fell for each other right away, but it was a while before we started dating exclusively. I was also dating a French restaurateur at the time, who had a restaurant in St. Bart's. He was really only proficient in restaurant English—"How is your meal?" "Where are you from?" "Have a good trip." So when I'd go down to visit him, Howard would court me by faxing love notes written in business English. He'd send a fax that said, "Are you available for a meeting in Napa next weekend?"—and that's how he would ask for a date, right under the chef's nose.

It wasn't long, though, before we were completely devoted to each other. Howard was everything I wanted in a man. He was witty, creative, and smart. He was a venture capitalist with a degree from the Harvard Business School—my fantasy Harvard guy at last. And this was the big thing: He was interested in what I had to say. He didn't think the world revolved around him. I had never been out with a guy I could sit and talk to for hours and hours. There was room for both of us in his life.

I was also struck immediately by two of this man's rare assets: his smiles. There was the smarty-ass smile, the one he indulged when he was having a little fun. But there was also the shy smile, the window into his sweeter, more vulnerable self. I loved them both.

Howard was centered and confident, and didn't have to be boastful because he was sure of who he was. He was a decent man, a good man, the kind you could make a home with. And I could see that right away. I was in my thirties by now, and the high life—jetting off to the Caribbean to meet my French boyfriend for an exotic weekend—was losing its appeal. When Howard came along, I had finally found something (someone) solid and rewarding to replace it with.

After a decade's worth of bad male behavior, though, I was still a little sensitive about just how much game-playing I would put up with. One late evening, after a full dose of dinner, dancing, and a lot of talk, Howard got up and announced abruptly that he had to go. His father's beach house had been broken into the night before, he said, and he'd promised to check and make sure everything was okay on his way home. I admired his conscientiousness—but I couldn't believe that he'd walk out on me so suddenly. To add insult to my injury, he left a smarmy little note on my windshield, saying how hard it was to leave, and that he "missed me already."

Of course, his father's house really *had* been broken into; I knew that. But at the same time that little windshield note just struck me as a trick out of Leave Them Wanting 101. I felt as if I'd been played. All through the next day I walked around fuming; finally I phoned him, and I could tell he thought his note would have hit a home run with this dainty little Southern belle. I lit into him like Scarlett O'Horror.

It was definitely a turning point in our relationship. The other day we were remembering this story, and Howard said: "The South has two sides to it. Everything is as sweet as peach pie—until it's not. You really went after me for that. 'What kind of amateur game are you playing with me, leaving a little note saying *It's so hard to leave*? If this is some kind of little sophomoric game, I'm not into it.' And you hung up. I felt like I'd just had my head snapped back like a boxer."

But the most remarkable thing was the effect speaking my mind had on Howard. "At that moment I knew I had to marry you," he says. "Any woman who could carry off all that intelligence and toughness with such grace—I thought, that's someone I can't let go."

The truth is, until that point in his life Howard had always been able to get away with whatever he wanted. Now he was faced with a woman who knew how to stand her ground without losing her femininity. He loved that. And I loved that he loved it.

Was this, you know, *it?* We thought so, but we were *so* cautious about crossing that line. Howard and I went to Italy together, our favorite holiday getaway, and had the most romantic time imaginable. We'd spend the day touring old churches and ruins, have long, sensual dinners, drink the most exquisite wine—even if it was really only everyday Italian table wine—and tell each other we just had to get married. One night we even asked our waiter if he knew of any place to get married that wasn't a Catholic church (and that's not so easy to find in Italy). And yet the next morning, in the harsh light of day, one of us would back off.

I guess for me the turning point came one evening back in Los Angeles, while we were having dinner at his place. Howard turned to me and said, "I have a feeling that I might be the one to end this relationship, before you do."

"Why on earth would you say something like that?" I said.

"Because I think I'm closer to the point—I'm not there now, but I'm close—where I'm ready to settle down with a life partner, to get married and have a family. I think I'm farther down that road than you are. And if I get there before you, that's when I'm going to turn to you and say, 'Well, this was a lot of fun, but I really need to be with somebody ready to take that step.'"

I was stunned. It's usually the woman who says, *I'm ready to get married and start a family, so it's time for you to fish or cut bait.* But now I was having the tables turned. This was something entirely new to me. But he was the kindest, most self-assured man I'd ever been with,

and by now I was old enough to know the real thing when I saw it.

I may have been headlong in love by that point, but I knew I still needed to get Howard down to Mississippi to see the family, to learn about who I am and where I hail from. He was a Jewish guy who grew up in L.A.; what he knew about the South came from books and movies—that it was the place where the Civil War was fought, where slavery was born and died, and where if the heat didn't kill you, the mosquitoes surely would.

We had a little work to do in the manners department, but he did fine, and they all loved him. He was a good sport about the funny accents, my father's obsession with the Weather Channel, and the many other eccentric customs we Southerners have. He knew how much my family and home means to me, so he learned to love it from the beginning. Years later he would tell me, "I didn't realize until I got to know the South how much of what I love in you comes from there."

As eager as he seemed, we danced around the question of marriage for what seemed like an eternity, until Howard confessed what was troubling him: He had his concerns about marrying an actress. Between the schedules, which could take me seven thousands of miles away for months at a time, and the on-camera love scenes, he just wasn't sure this was what he had in mind for his married life.

But at long last we ran out of reasons to wait. We were in Manhattan one weekend afternoon just before Christmas, having cappuccino at Bistro Ferrier, a quiet little Upper East Side café off Madison Avenue, when he took a small box out of his pocket and put it on the table.

"Honey," he said, "I'm giving you this because I love you."

I opened the box, and there was a ring inside: rose gold, with tiny diamonds all around. Howard said nothing else, so I put it on, and told him how sweet he was.

He took out a second box. It was a matching ring, this time in white gold. "I'm giving you this because I love every minute I'm with you," he said. I smiled and put it on, still not sure what was going on.

Then he pulled out a third box, yellow gold this time. He said, "And I'm giving you this because I want to marry you."

There, he had said it. I gazed across the table at this beautiful man, this big-hearted soul with whom I wanted nothing more than to spend the rest of my life. He was the secret wish of my heart since I was a little girl, the man I wanted to be the father of my children, my first and my last, my true love. And this was our moment. I lost myself in his gaze.

I didn't realize it until he told me later, but I just looked at him, without saying a word, for what Howard calls "the longest two minutes in my life." As he sat there, sweating buckshot, thinking I was trying to find a way to let him down easy after my two minutes of silence, I brought my hand out from under the table and gave him a box.

"Open this," I said.

Howard thought I didn't understand what was happening. He was feeling confused, vulnerable, and angry; at that point all he wanted was for me to make the rejection quick and painless. Silently he scrambled to plan his getaway: the restaurant check, the immediate flight back to L.A., the quick transition from planned euphoria to unplanned disaster. I could see the emotion all over his face.

"Just open the box," I said.

Inside was a Bulgari watch. "Thank you," Howard said, taken aback. "But maybe I didn't make myself clear. We're not exchanging presents here."

"Would you turn it over, please?" I said softly.

These words were engraved on the back of the timepiece: *Yes. My love forever. Sela.*

Howard was stunned. His anger melted away. "How long have you been carrying this watch?" he asked.

"I've had it on me twenty-four hours a day since that moment I told you I was ready," I said.

And so we were engaged.

Strangely enough, I didn't call Mama and Daddy to tell them until after I had brunch with my sister, Jenna, the next day. I didn't know how they would react. But Jenna made us march to the phone booth in the back of the restaurant, where I called Mama to give her the news. She told Daddy; then I put Howard on the phone to tell him personally.

Howard delivered the news to his future father-in-law, who responded with typical taciturnity: "Well, that's what I've been hearing. Howard, you'll have to excuse me a second. It takes me a while to get used to these big things. Kind of like death."

And then he said, without missing a beat, "Tell Sela I changed the oil in her Barracuda."

Reader, that's my daddy. And I love him to pieces.

We had an engagement party with about two hundred people down at Boyette's Fish Camp on the Chunky River. Howard stood up and told the crowd that he didn't know if he was at his own engagement party or at a convention of salesmen, because he'd never been around so many people who were so genuinely friendly. "Normally when you're around so many friendly people, they're trying to sell you something," Howard joked. It was his first true megadose of Southern hospitality.

As we started planning the wedding, I found myself having something of a personal crisis. Howard is Jewish, and I began to worry about having an interfaith marriage. We agreed that we would raise our kids knowing about both sides of their religious heritage, but they would be primarily Jewish. But I began to have doubts that I was doing the right thing. I went to Dr. Apperson, my childhood pastor, to seek his counsel.

He said to me, "You know what, Sela? I believe you can find God in the temple on Friday night just as easily as you can in church on Sunday morning." With Dr. Apperson's blessing, I knew I was ready to marry the man I loved.

Dr. Apperson died two years ago. Before he passed away, I wrote him a note to let him know what a gift he gave me, raising me in a church that wore its dogma lightly, so that I wouldn't feel like a traitor to the faith for marrying a man of another religion. Had that dear old pastor not given me his blessing, I might have missed out on God's three greatest gifts to me: Howard, and our two children. I told Dr. Apperson: "You gave me that gift." And I meant it with all my heart.

We considered having the wedding in my church in Meridian, but we didn't have anywhere special there to have the reception. The beautiful country club that had been modeled after George Washington's home at Mount Vernon had been torn down, and replaced with an uninviting modern building that looked like a nondescript Colorado ski chalet. So instead we decided to marry outdoors at my dear friend Martee Snider's gorgeous estate in Montecito. Daddy drove out in my Barracuda, which may be the strangest dowry any California bride has ever presented to her husband.

I probably had more fun on our wedding day—May 23, 1992—than on any other day of my life—though I had to shake off a few jitters along the way. I had a manicure scheduled, and a massage, but I was so nervous I couldn't bring myself to relax. As I was having my makeup done, though, all my girlfriends from out of town stopped by to say hello, and just their presence helped put me at ease. When the time came for the ceremony to begin I took my place at Daddy's

side, standing in the rear of the house. Howard and the ministers—
my Episcopal priest cousin Tom, and a rabbi—stood under a chuppah in the distance, with the pond and the mountains in the
background. We'd given Martee a pair of swans in thanks for letting
us use her home, and she'd named them Howard and Sela; they
were swimming in the background as we were married. It was quite
a production: As I walked down a white runner some two hundred
yards long to reach the chuppah, I thought, "Only an actress would
do this."

Me being me, I would normally have looked around as I walked down the aisle to make sure everybody was in place, that all was well, that Mama was doing fine. But I didn't. I never took my eyes off Howard. We stood there before God and our families and friends, and pledged our lives to each other. It was perfect. We didn't have a formal recessional; rather, everyone went straightaway to a black-and-white checkered dance floor we'd set up, and started dancing to the Motown band. Sweet soul music was one of the joys of my life as a girl, so it seemed right that the curtain would come down on my youth with such an exuberant fanfare. Marvin, Aretha, Al, Smokey, and the rest had seen me through so much joy and heartache. It was only right that they should be there to serenade me as I stepped into the next act of my life.

I think about that happy, happy woman, dancing in the strong arms of her new husband on that warm spring day under the California sky, and I smile. She did not know, she could not have known, that her long flight from her homeland was ending that day. She knew she was no longer a jet-setter, that she was a wife now. And she hoped she would soon be a mother. What would that mean to her? She could only guess.

But she was also a Southerner—and soon she would want to be one in more than name only. You know those birds you send off, the ones that always find their way back? The bride had been out flying high for many, many years, and she was about to learn that it was time to head home to rest.

God gave all men all earth to love
But since our hearts are small
Ordained for each one spot should
prove
Beloved over all.

—RUDYARD KIPLING

The Rose Cottage,
Honeysuckle Farms.

6 ⟫

They say that once you marry and start a family, you start to return to your own childhood, consciously or not. And that's what happened for me, in a big way. Our wedding was in May, and by December we'd already begun digging our toes back into the Southern soil.

That first summer as husband and wife, Howard and I were still living *la vida loca*, traveling a lot, eating dinner out every night, making the most of our newlywed life. But we were also in our midthirties, and the urge to make life a nonstop romantic adventure was something we'd both gotten pretty much out of our system. We were both ready to start building something solid and lasting. Before long I was telling Howard that it would be nice if we could give our kids (*Kids!* We'd been married a month!) a taste of home down South.

At first Howard just listened, a little bemused. "It was like that six-month honeymoon period new presidents have, where Congress gives them the leeway to pass new legislation," he told me recently. "I just thought, 'Sure, honey, whatever you want.' I was determined for you to think you'd married the greatest guy in the world. I didn't want you to have buyer's remorse. It seemed to me that you had this *Field of Dreams* fantasy: if we built the farm, everything else would come."

By "building the farm," what Howard meant was a dream I'd been quietly cultivating for years, mostly unawares, but which now was breaking happily through to the surface. I wanted to go back to Meridian, at last. To take my husband and our children there, to expose us all to the fresh air and soil and good people of the land where I'd been raised.

I hadn't realized, until I was married, how powerful this impulse within me had grown to be. But I know that for years I had always loved the idea of a family compound—not so much a lavish, Kennedy-style family seat, but a decent parcel of land where my family could gather and enjoy the countryside together. I'd grown tired of vacation spots; I wanted not just a place to get away from it all, but a place that was a destination all its own. I'd been to the home of one of Berry's friends, whose family had a kind of enclave in the country outside of Meridian; I remembered our riding horses down a dirt road there, under the canopy of oak trees, and just thinking, *This is perfect.* And that image stayed with me long enough that eventually I realized it wasn't just an idle whim—it was something I needed.

"What I didn't know was that once we found a place, you'd want to go there every time you had ten minutes away from work," Howard says, laughing. "If I'd known we'd be spending 80 percent of our vacations in one spot, I might have suggested a flat in Paris."

But he never got the chance. Right away I enlisted Daddy's help as a land scout, and before we knew it he'd found the perfect tract of land, a hilly spread that had once been a dairy farm. "This real estate man showed me all over the country outside of Meridian," Daddy says. "As soon as we came upon this place, it looked like heaven, almost. The minute I saw it, I said, 'You don't have to go anywhere else, I'm going to call her and tell her I found the place.'" We call it Honeysuckle Farms.

As soon as we'd made it ours, we started planning. One ideal building site on the land was already occupied, by a dilapidated old fishing shack next to one of the ponds; the building itself wasn't really worth saving, but it had a gorgeous old redbrick chimney, and we decided to rescue it so that we could build our new home around an old hearth. Interior design is a passion of mine, so the chance to design our new cottage from scratch was a dream come true. But what kind of place did I want? It needed to be practical enough to house the family Howard and I wanted to have, but also dreamy enough to fulfill my desire for a serene country retreat, a sacred space where I could soothe my city-battered soul. I wanted this little house to feel embracing and comforting, to be not just a spare vacation cabin but a home that expressed my personality. What's more, I wanted the décor to be visibly Southern, so my guests from points north and west would be swept away by the sense of place—and, for that matter, so would I.

Just as soon as we'd gotten started, of course, our wish list got away from us. We wanted a master bedroom; we wanted a suite for Mama and Daddy; we wanted a suite for Jenna to use when she came home. We wanted sleeping porches for kids, once we had them. We wanted a gym, a study that could double as a screening room, and a great room for entertaining. But when an architect friend drew up some plans that accommodated all our wishes, we saw with astonishment that our little starter home had mushroomed to ten thousand square feet—hardly the cozy cottage of our dreams. So we shelved those plans for the time being, and decided to start small.

The design Howard and I finally settled on could hardly have been more simple. Our little shingled cottage is essentially a one-room structure, modeled after the San Ysidro Ranch cottage where we spent our honeymoon night. It's dominated by our brick hearth, with a little bathroom off the back, and a nook-size children's bedroom as well. The kitchen wraps around behind the hearth. We gave it a big screen porch, deep enough to host dinner parties on; fronted it with a creaky screen door; bookended it with porch swings; and filled it with rocking chairs looking out over the pond. And we garlanded the front with a lush, flowering English garden full of azaleas, gardenias, and roses. We Southerners have always had a soft spot for all things English. At the time I was reading a romantic novel (by Rosamunde Pilcher, I think), in which the author described an English countryside manor where each bedroom was named after a different flower. I was so taken by the romance of the idea that I decided our getaway place would be called the Rose Cottage.

For the interior I cobbled together a look that was floral and feminine. I spent weekends in New Orleans buying art objects, antique furniture, and other Victoriana from auction galleries. I kept my eye out for special pieces that were historically faithful to the antebellum South. And I had some lucky finds: four-poster canopy beds and music stands to use as end tables, nineteenth-century botanical prints (roses, of course) to line the walls, and rose-shaped iron finials to crown the posts at the base of the cottage stoop. A pair of highly polished men's riding boots I fell in love with sit beside a venerable-looking writing desk, with an antique chair I found in L.A. (The dealer swore he'd bought it from Elliott Gould, and that it had belonged to him and Barbra Streisand; I guess I just needed a little taste of Hollywood, even here.)

And as we finished off the inside of the cottage, we also added a few homey amenities to the grounds: hammocks and Adirondack chairs scattered about near the house, birdhouses in the trees, and a fishing pier on the pond. We even built a little island in the pond for the waterfowl, covered it with azalea bushes and a gazebo, and joined it to the bank with a white wooden arched bridge. Every evening we spent down there in those early days, we repaired to the porch to gaze out at our slice of heaven: weeping willows frame the view of the pond, and lazy ducks, swans, and geese glide on the pond till darkness falls.

Two years after we finished the Rose Cottage, we completed a second cabin nearby. Less ornamented, more rustic, this two-bedroom cottage was dubbed the Cotton Patch, after a charming country restaurant outside Tuscaloosa I'd loved during my college years. We planted a real cotton patch out front by the gravel road, and now my children love picking it and taking it back to school in Los Angeles for show-and-tell.

I still look forward to building a big house here one day; as a hopeless romantic, I think of it as my Tara. But for now we're deliriously happy in this pair of pocket-size dwellings. The Rose Cottage and the Cotton Patch: together they're a home away from home, a sanctuary, a nurturing space where I can be still and at rest and one with the land. It took a lot of patience and introspection to pull together the elements of this physical environment, and I took no end of pleasure in the process. But it takes more than just interior decoration to make a sacred space like this. The magic I feel when we arrive at the cottages after a long stretch in the city, I think, has less to do with what Howard and I have built here physically than with what we want to build here spiritually. It takes in so many deeper wishes of mine: to carve out a safe and sane place to raise my family. To immerse us all in surroundings that are quieter, gentler, more natural and unhurried. To maintain a connection with the people I love, and the land of my raising. And above all to have a place, as Ellis Peters wrote, "where I put my feet up and thank God."

It was in 1993, while we were building the Rose Cottage, that Howard and I decided we should try to have a baby. It was the most frightening decision I had ever made, because it was so fraught with responsibility, and so irrevocable. How did I know I would be a good mother? I didn't; nobody does. I was terrified about how our life together would change. Remember, I was thirty-five when I got married, and I'd been used to living carefree, able to stay as late as I wanted at dinner or take off on a last-minute vacation if the yen struck. Once you have kids, all that freedom evaporates in a flurry of diapers and tiny shoes.

But any concerns about my freedom paled in the face of that

much stronger, more visceral urge—to start a family. I thank God I had the courage to make that decision, for if I hadn't I would have missed out on the most incredible journey of my life. There's an enigmatic Tamil saying that speaks to my feelings: "Children tie their mother's feet down." The ambiguity is the key: though its message can seem like a curse (*My children hold me back; I'll never fly again*), for me the truer meaning is that children anchor you more firmly to the earth. For this mother, who spent so many years floating wherever the winds of whim would take her, children have been nothing but a blessing.

Childbearing opened my heart in a way I had never imagined. During Austin's birth I don't remember sobbing the way I expected to; I just remember being stunned and mesmerized by the miracle of the experience. In the days thereafter, everyday life took on the vividness of Technicolor. I began having intense emotional reactions to everything; even sappy television commercials seemed so moving I couldn't keep from crying. It was as though a light had just been turned on in my life.

Aside from the gaga moments, there were some pretty absurd times, too. Howard and I had both reached early middle age without ever changing a diaper. As we strapped Austin's car seat into the back of the car at the hospital, we looked at each other and said, "Can you believe they're letting us take this kid home?!"

To be honest, though, amid the flood of love I felt for Austin, in those first days of his life I also felt overwhelmed by another emotion: fear. Of course I had the natural instincts—to nurture him, protect him, give everything I had to this new creature. But there was a deep-seated part of me that wondered at first whether I was really fully equipped to handle the job. Every time I turned around, it seemed, there was some new challenge: *What did that cry mean? Will he stop breath-*

With Austin

ing? What about crib death? Will he ever learn to walk and talk? But I had eight glorious weeks to spend with Austin, uninterrupted, before I had to be back to work, and in that time I seemed to find my footing.

Three years later I was pregnant again, and not for a single moment did I doubt that this time I was going to have a girl. Something told me I was supposed to experience the mother-daughter relationship. Finally my own diagnosis was confirmed: "Well, we've got the tests back," the doctor called to say, "and you should start buying pink." I screamed! I was so happy. We named her Anabella Raye, after my cigar-smoking, fudge-making grandmother.

. . . . and Annabella

So from the beginning, then, my two children and my rekindled love for my small-town home have grown together. Austin's first trip to Meridian came just weeks after he was born, and four years later Anabella followed as soon as she was old enough to travel by plane. My emotional compass has shifted southeast as they've grown, and I'm doing everything I can to help them find in Meridian the same home comforts their mother does.

In some ways it hasn't really felt like a major lifestyle upheaval. Despite my eagerness to leave home at eighteen, I'd never missed a Christmas in Meridian, or a chance to meet the family for a vacation on the Gulf. Of course, I'd done a lot of traveling in my twenties, when I had the chance—who wouldn't? But no place else is home, and every time I returned the sight of these humble hills and red-clay hollows became dearer to me than I could possibly express.

It wasn't only the look of the land that drew me back, of course; it was Mama and Daddy. It was my brother Berry, who stayed in Meridian to start his own family when the rest of us kids left. What had always restored me on my trips back home was the time I spent together with them. It was good, honest time: stopping by Weidmann's for an early breakfast with Daddy; long, slow Saturday afternoons spent talking with Mama. Once Howard and I started our family, I guess my heart just reached right out to those memories. I was eager to share them with Austin and Anabella. And, I have to admit, I was anxious about the notion that if I didn't take care, my children might never get to know this part of me—and of themselves.

My anxiety sprang, in large part, from the misgivings I'd started having about life in the city, where my children would, of necessity, spend most of their young lives.

From the start, Howard understood my concerns—despite, or perhaps because of, what he remembered from his own childhood. Howard was raised in a small Los Angeles suburb, in what sounds in some ways like an idyllic little neighborhood: lots of other kids around, basketball hoops in the yard, the works. But when he looks back on his childhood, he doesn't feel that same warm flush of memories come over him. "Growing up here in L.A.," he says, "you don't feel like you have a home, or are part of anything."

One reason may be the schedule he kept. Howard was a precocious little kid, and his parents kept him on a pretty fast treadmill; he was into sports in a big way, along with piano, painting, guitar, and Hebrew school, all while racking up a series of grades that, after third grade, never dipped lower than an A. I don't know how he did it—I

would have felt as if I were in training for an ulcer. But with the culture of play dates and after-school classes now fully entrenched around the country, of course I know that my kids' lives won't be too different.

My Uncle Joe marvels at this kind of social-calendar childhood. "These kids have their mamas taking 'em here, taking them there. Back when I was a kid, if we wanted to get somewhere, we had to walk there ourselves—or we had a bicycle or something, you know. Yeah, if I'd had to depend on a car I'd have been up a creek."

Talking with Uncle Joe, you get a real picture of how small-town childhood used to be. "We lived right across the street from the fairgrounds," he remembers, "and there was a playground down there. You know, we didn't have organized sports in school. But we couldn't get out of the house early enough in the morning to get our own game going. Kept it going all day long. I mean, we weren't staying in the house and watching TV—we didn't even *have* TV. We were out there playing ball all day, or playing hockey in the streets, you know, on roller skates. We didn't even want to go in and eat lunch—Mama had to call us in. You entertained yourself. You didn't have anybody organizing you. You did it yourself."

Recently I came across a book called *Bowling Alone: The Collapse and Revival of American Community,* and so much of what it had to say rang true to me as I thought about the lives children lead in a city like Los Angeles. Before I read it, I often wondered: *Am I just succumbing to false nostalgia?* But the author, a sociologist named Robert D. Putnam, confirmed my impression—that our communities were more . . . well, *communal* before and during the years of my childhood than they would become soon thereafter.

"For the first two-thirds of the 20th century," Putnam writes, "a powerful tide bore Americans into ever deeper engagement in the life of their communities, but a few decades ago—silently, without warning—that tide reversed, and we were overtaken by a treacherous rip current. Without at first noticing, we have been pulled apart from one another and our communities over the last third of the century."

Americans in our parents' and grandparents' day, it seems, were different from us in at least one key respect: They weren't embarrassed to *belong* to something. They belonged to clubs, to teams, to civic groups: to the Kiwanis, the Rotary, the Elks; to the Ladies' Auxiliary or a church group or the local bowling league. Sometime around 1968, though—just before I became a teenager—Americans started looking elsewhere for entertainment, and I guess even for our sense of identity. We Baby Boomers were a youthful and headstrong bunch, and it seems as though many of us were more interested in our personal lives and pursuits than we were in spending our time with the older generations who populated the American Legion halls and bingo nights at church.

And it wasn't just a matter of belonging to clubs. So many of us Boomers grew up in suburban developments, which sprang up like weeds out of any available topsoil in the years after World War II. More than half of all Americans live in the suburbs today, but they're difficult places to become attached to, and they're not exactly fertile ground for meaningful social relationships. As social critic James Howard Kunstler writes in his book *The Geography of Nowhere*, "A suburbanite could stand on her lawn for three hours on a weekday afternoon and never have the chance for a conversation." With no ceremonial buildings nearby to lend a sense of history or community, and no mom-and-pop shops to become informal gathering spots for the neighborhood, they're less likely to foster a sense of pride or loyalty than to breed disaffection.

In that respect, among so many others, I count myself lucky. The little Lakemont enclave of my childhood sprang up during the suburban boom, to be sure. Yet in its particulars—the shared interests with the neighbors, the access to nature, and the proximity of our extended family—I think it had more in common with that older way of life than the second- and third-generation suburbs so many of our children are growing up in today. Perhaps that's one reason that my yearnings for home are so strong: the time I grew up was one of transition, when the old ways were still vivid, not yet fully transplanted by the new.

As Joe mentioned, childhood has changed in one other respect: Where our parents grew up playing on their parents' porches after dinner, our children are growing up behind the picture window, watching television. A friend of mine was telling me not long ago how the coming of television changed the rural community where he grew up. His parents and their friends used to get together for barbecues and fish fries all the time, he recalls; their summer socializing often revolved around their kids' sporting events, and fall and winter get-togethers were built around men bringing in game from the woods.

"When we kids grew up and left home, and the men slowed down on the hunting, that was pretty much it for the community," my friend laments. "It's so sad to see what's happened. My folks and their friends almost never see each other anymore. Everybody's at home watching satellite TV, which we didn't have then. They got out of the habit of seeing each other, and finally they just lost interest."

Los Angeles, of course, is a big city. But to me, in all these respects, it feels like the ultimate suburb. New York can be a pretty harrowing place to live, but at least it's still a walking city—a collec-

tion of human-scale neighborhoods strung together by sidewalks and subways. Move into a new neighborhood, and before you know it you'll recognize half the people you see on your walk to work in the morning. And, as anyone who grew up in Brooklyn can tell you, New York is still full of people who take pride in where they're from.

In L.A., on the other hand, sometimes it seems like everyone's a transplant. It's an industry town, and that industry—show business— draws ambitious people in from all over the country. (By now, I'll bet *all* of them were born and raised in the suburbs.) It's a driving city; you don't see much of anybody on the way to work—not through the tinted glass of their sports cars on the highway. And outside of a small (but noble) group of Hollywood-history buffs and L.A. boosters, there's not much sense of community. You see big thinkers endlessly chewing over this problem in the pages of the city's papers, but nobody seems to know what to do about it. Most residents' sense of identity comes from how successful their careers are, not where they live, and the social networking they do is typically motivated by self-interest, not civic interest. And it's not only happening in L.A.

That's a recipe for alienation—and it's a kind of alienation that is leaving too many of us, in Los Angeles and elsewhere, unfulfilled. "The single most common finding from a half-century's research on the [causes of] life satisfaction, not only in the United States but around the world," Robert Putnam writes, "is that happiness is best predicted by the breadth and depth of one's social connections."

Los Angeles, in short, is a place of great material and creative wealth, and boundless personal freedom—but also of a certain spiritual and civic poverty. Though there are many wonderful people here, on the whole it's an anxious, self-involved place, where roots and tradition are largely forgotten, where neighbors don't know each other and don't particularly want to. It's not that L.A. people are bad, but that there's something about the way life is structured in this sunny paradise that leaves people feeling atomized and power-less to do anything about our common condition.

I know it. I feel it myself, and had been feeling it for a long time before I realized how homesick I was. And I want better for my children.

I also want to be a better parent for them than I feel I always am back in L.A.

I think about this a lot, in part because Austin and Anabella are still young enough that I *can* learn to be better for them. Every hour I spend with them—Austin playing with his first basketball, Anabella basking in the delight of a new toy or some new idea she wants to share with me—is an education for me in what children are like, in what they need in life, in what they need from me.

The most dangerous part of trying to raise kids in a place like Hollywood—it's the biggest occupational hazard of show business, but I think it's equally popular nationwide—is something pretty simple: self-absorption. We Baby Boomers are an unusually intense lot. We work hard, desperate to make something of ourselves, to ful-fill our ambitions and creative dreams, to provide for our families and put enough away for our retirement. We also play hard, some-times as hard as our kids; as much as we try to save money, we're just as eager to spend it on new gadgets, SUVs, endless computer upgrades, meals at fabulous new restaurants, home improvements, and all kinds of other indulgences. And there's nothing wrong with any of this, not really: it's the American dream, after all, to work hard and then enjoy what you've earned.

But all of that time spent at hard work and hard play can come at the expense of something else: time. With all the extra hours we put in, trying to provide a better life for ourselves and our kids, too often we're forgetting that the only really important thing we can give them is time together. Our kids are supposed to have us around as much as possible. We're their earliest playmates, their first and best teachers, their role models. In a way that's hard for adults to remember, children are exquisitely attuned to the signals we send them. They're looking for affirmation, for comfort, for reassurance that we care about them. And even if we have the best caretakers in the world for our children, every moment we spend away from them is a missed opportunity to remind them of our love, and marvel in their uniqueness.

Among the gifts my parents gave us, perhaps the richest was time together as a family. With that, I realize now, came the unwavering awareness that we were loved, not just by our parents but by the extended family that was constantly within reach. My parents always loved having their brothers and sisters around; for us kids, that meant a reliable source of laps to sit on, and cousins to play with. There wasn't a need my parents had that they couldn't find some family member to help with, whether it was picking up the kids or making Sunday dinner. And, like their own before them, my parents realized that taking care of the older generation was both a blessing and a responsibility. "My grandmother," Uncle Joe remembers, "when she got old and frail, came and lived with my family when we three boys all got called in the Korean War. Then my *mother*, as she got older, you know, came and lived with you, Sela, and your family." Having such close contact with the generations was a family tradition—and though it would be harder to do from California, it was one I wanted dearly not to break.

Raising kids in a two-career family is hard, as Howard and I know all too well. Howard's work keeps him at the office till the middle of the evening, and when I'm working—which has been pretty much constantly since I got the role on *Sisters*—I usually come in that late or later. When I started work on the series *Once & Again* a few years ago I negotiated a promise from the producers to grant me more time with my kids during filming. But it worked better in theory than in practice, and too often I found myself leaving for the set before they woke up and not returning until they were off to bed. This is no way to live—certainly not for extended periods. I don't want my children to reach adulthood with their most vivid memories of their mother being images they remember from television. And I'll admit to a selfish motivation, too: I don't want to wake up one day and realize I've missed my children's childhood in a haze of 6:00 A.M. calls and late-night retakes. As the saying goes, nobody lies on their deathbed wishing they'd spent more time at the office.

I'm also concerned about making sure my children have enough direction in their lives, and enough discipline. After a long stretch away from home, I have a tendency to play the good cop when I come back, because I want Austin and Anabella to like me when they have me around. There's a strong temptation to overindulge them, to let them get away with things even when I know it's not the best thing for them, because I don't want to be the Big Mean Mommy. I think about laying down stricter rules for them, but they're both so well behaved that it's easy to carry on assuming that everything's going fine. In Austin's preschool years I started worrying about whether he'd become one of the overindulged children

TV seems to promise us all, yelling and screaming, ignoring his parents, inhaling candy, and talking pop-culture trash. *Will my kids turn out that way?* I wondered. I don't think they have—at least, not yet. But how can I make sure they stay that way?

One day when I was at a dinner party I found myself talking about all this, and I discovered that the brilliant woman seated next to me had made these very issues her calling. Wendy Mogel, a local psychologist, had come to realize that the problem many families were suffering from wasn't a matter of psychology, exactly, but of something much simpler: character. Wendy herself had begun feeling that she was failing her girls and her husband, that she didn't have enough time for them and wasn't raising them as responsibly as she should, until she began to explore elements of the Jewish faith and moral tradition—a legacy her secular Jewish parents hadn't endeavored to share with her. When she began integrating traditional religious approaches into her child and family counseling—and into her own family life—she found it brought about surprisingly effective results.

This sounded intriguing, so I asked Wendy to send me a copy of her book, *The Blessing of a Skinned Knee.* And when I read this passage, early in the book, I nearly gasped:

> Unsure how to find grace and security in the complex world we've inherited, we try to fill up the spaces in our children's lives with stuff: birthday entertainments, lessons, rooms full of toys and equipment, tutors and therapists. But material pleasures can't buy peace of mind, and all the excess leads to more anxiety. . . . In their eagerness to do right by

their children, parents not only overindulge them materially, they also spoil them emotionally. Many parents have unhappy memories of their own childhoods, of not being allowed to express their feelings or participate in decisions. In trying to undo these past violations, they move too far in the other direction—they overvalue their children's need for self-expression and turn their households into little democracies. But the equality they maintain at home does not give their children a sense of self-esteem. Instead, it frightens them by sending the message that their parents are not firmly in charge. By refusing to be authority figures, these parents don't empower their children, they make them insecure.

Wendy goes on to say that parents these days often "fetishize their children's achievements and feelings and neglect to help them develop a sense of duty to others." Moms and dads are so worried that their children are going to be hurt emotionally or physically that they shelter the kids, protecting them from the everyday scrapes with reality that help them build character (hence the book's title). What's more, well-meaning parents set their children up for anxiety and failure by overloading them with unrealistic expectations, whether academic, athletic, or artistic—inadvertently turning the kids into "emblems of their parents' success," rather than allowing them the breathing room to lead their own lives.

Did this strike a chord within me? I'm afraid so. And the truth is, despite whatever romantic illusions I'd like to preserve in my own mind, even the South hasn't escaped this phenomenon. "We get a lot of the same thing here now," my brother Berry tells me. "Kids don't have any respect anymore. Their parents spoil them rotten.

"Used to be when we were kids, if we got in trouble at school, or our grades were down, Mama would go in to see the teacher, wanting to know how she could help us improve," he says. "Nowadays, if you can get the parents to go in at all, they show up wanting to know why the school is picking on their child. You don't think kids learn from that? They come away thinking the world owes them. It's a shame to see it, because you know our generation wasn't raised that way."

My Aunt Nancy says the same thing. She sees it as a loss of Christian values among newer generations of Southerners, but for all practical purposes she's talking about the same thing Wendy Mogel is. What I take away from all their perspectives—Wendy's, Berry's, Aunt Nancy's—is that we have to find a path back to a more balanced, considerate, sane way to raise kids. Whether the inspiration comes from Jewish tradition, Christian values, or our shared human awareness of the difference between right and wrong, the effect we're all looking for is the same. We want to be good to our children—not overindulgent, not overdemanding, but nurturing and helpful and gently encouraging. We want them to learn the best qualities from us—to give them the tools to grow up and become good and fulfilled and happy people themselves.

Wendy Mogel talks about three core principles that have guided her down this path: moderation, celebration, and sanctification. In a nutshell, she means that if we want to have happy, healthy homes, then we have to learn—both individually and within our families—to practice self-discipline, to cultivate a genuinely grateful spirit, and to get in the habit of recognizing the sacred in our daily lives.

After all, she says, the more our kids are aware of a higher power, the less likely they'll be to think that they rule the world.

This sounds wise and good, but it is hard to do in a world where all the people seem to be out for themselves, and there's little shared moral understanding among parents in any given community.

What a far cry from the world of my mother's generation. Aunt Nancy told me once, "When I was raising kids, and we saw other people's children doing something bad, we wouldn't have hesitated to correct them. There was more of a community feeling then. Those children knew they'd better not act up, because an adult was watching them. My kids knew better, because they knew I'd back up any adult who disciplined them."

For me, there's nothing that crystallizes this cultural shift better than what I call the Yes, Sir–No, Ma'am dilemma. In my childhood—whether you were four, fourteen, or forty—it would have been unthinkable to address your elders as anything other than "sir" or "ma'am." But a Southern-born parent raising kids elsewhere today faces a tricky little challenge: Do you teach your children to use the more respectful Southern form of address when speaking to grown-ups, or to follow the manners of the society in which they actually live? I know of a Louisiana woman living in Santa Monica whose daughter was regularly corrected by a teacher—and mocked by her classmates—because she addressed the teacher as "ma'am." When the mother asked for an explanation, the teacher responded that the girl's polite little habit was threatening classroom order—not to mention drawing a lot of negative attention from the other kids. Realizing how little choice she had in the matter, the mother gave in.

But it wasn't a happy experience—and I know how she felt. My son, Austin, attends a good elementary school in California, where he's getting a wonderful education from dedicated teachers. But there's one rule they practice that will always sit wrong with me: The children call their teachers by their first names. It's hard to describe the sense of defilement—that's a strong word, but I think it's the right one—that native Southerners feel when they observe children addressing adults this way. And when it's your own children doing it, it's like feeling you've sent them out into the world with dirty faces.

But the alternative—insisting on a code of manners from a place not their own—is cruel. That's something I've simply had to accept. Still, I'm trying to teach them to switch languages, so to speak, when we go down to Mississippi.

One Christmas not long after Anabella was born, the four of us were down in Meridian for the holiday, and I made a trip to a local Wal-Mart to buy Christmas presents for kids I didn't know. It was my habit to drop off gifts at the local shelter for abused children, where kids who have to be removed from their families stay before going to foster care.

When I got there, I saw some of the newest arrivals: a pair of brothers, African American boys, ages eight and nine. They had been taken out of their house in part because their father had been prostituting their eleven-year-old sister. Those boys had been through hell, but they still had such sweetness and promise in their faces. If they were lucky enough to be placed together, immediately, with a foster family who loved them and would take care of them, they might end up safe and happy. But it looked as if they were

Paula Merritt/The Meridian S

OVING EMBRACE — Girl Scout Dallas Riley of Meridian hugs Emmy Award-winning
tress Sela Ward after the official opening Thursday of Hope Village for Children. Ward, a
uderdale County native, was a driving force in development of the residence for abused
d neglected children at the former Masonic Home site on 23rd Avenue.

Wow!': Dream of Hope
Village becomes a reality

about to be split up and dumped into the overtaxed and dangerous foster-care system, where they would probably come out the other end cynical, angry, and maybe even destructive.

I thought: *I've got to save these children.*

I called Howard back at the farm. "We've got to adopt these two little boys," I told him, choking back a flood of tears.

"What?" he said.

These children had nobody, I told him. We had it within our power to save their lives, and I thought we should try.

"Sela, we struggle the same as everyone else to put love into that bucket-with-a-hole-in-it called our children," Howard said. "No matter how much love you put into it, it's never filled up. With our work schedules, and everything we've taken on in life, we don't have room to adopt two kids."

I knew he was right, but I didn't want to hear it. "There has to be something we could do for kids like this. We can't just walk away, can we, Howard?"

"Well, why don't we see if there's something we *can* do?" he said. "If the problem is that these kids don't have a permanent home to go to, then let's create one."

And that's what we did. First of all, atop a grassy hill in Meridian, we discovered an abandoned building that had once been an orphanage. I contacted my "angel," Lisa Paulsen of the Entertainment Industry Foundation, and she helped me broker a deal with Kentucky Fried Chicken to do an ad for them in exchange for money to buy the home and surrounding land. Within months renovations began on the building, and our dream had a home: Hope Village for Children, a permanent refuge for abused and abandoned kids.

Howard, who's not just a venture capitalist but a visionary, came up with the idea to make Hope Village more than just a safe and comfortable place for kids to live until they reach the age of majority. He suggested that we make it a "campus for the care of children." We could teach the kids all kinds of practical skills—the kinds of things more fortunate children learn from their parents. We could help them with their checkbooks, with college applications; then, after they leave, we'd still be available to offer them advice and guidance. What's more, we decided to document everything we were doing; if the model works, we intend to create Hope Villages across the country—a nonprofit franchise dedicated to rescuing children from a failing system.

Though we're still taking small steps, Hope Village is now a reality, and we have our first residents living there. As I write this, we're putting the finishing touches on an emergency shelter to house the littlest children, from newborn babies to twelve-year-olds; this will complement the services already under way in our permanent home, which serves six- to eighteen-year-olds. Every time I come home to Meridian I stop by to see the boys and girls in residence, and I end up feeling so small (in a good way), and useful, for once. The kinds of horrific things those children have seen and borne in their few years on this earth are things most of us spend a lifetime without encountering.

It might have been unrealistic, even unfair, for me to try to adopt those two little boys—or any of the millions of other vulnerable children living in our world today—and make my home their own. But through Hope Village for Children, I hope to do something more: to give them a home. Not an institution, not an orphanage, but a home.

I t's not the houses I love,
it's the life I live in them.

—Coco Chanel

Meridian is the 1950s—
the Weidmann's sign is visible on the right.

7 ☙

They say you can't go home again, but for the sake of our kids and the peace of my soul, Howard and I do the best we can. These days we travel down to Meridian five or six times a year. The city itself is mostly quiet now, its stately old buildings abandoned by shoppers when the malls started to open at the edge of town—just around the time, I realize, when I was heading north for New York.

It wasn't always this way, of course. At the turn of the twentieth century Meridian was a major regional center, with five railroad lines passing through town carrying forty passenger trains per day to what was known as Mississippi's Queen City. Two generations later, my Aunt Nancy remembers, the city was still hopping.

"Downtown was the heart of the whole community," she recalls.

"This was mostly an agricultural area then, and Saturday was the day all the farmers came into town for their shopping. That was the whole commercial district then, and you got to see everybody on the street on Saturday. It was very exciting. I can remember my mom taking me shopping to the nice department stores to buy clothes. It was such an event we would dress up for it."

In the last quarter-century, though, the streets and storefronts of Meridian have emptied, as new generations shifted their attention from the city to the suburbs. This is what James Howard Kunstler is writing about in *The Geography of Nowhere*: that the abandonment of downtowns, where everything you needed was pretty much within a ten-minute walk, has made us a nation of loners, craving connectedness but having nowhere to find it. Postwar suburban living, he writes, has "done away with the sacred places, places of casual public assembly, and places of repose. Otherwise, there remain only the shopping plazas, the supermarkets, and the malls," he writes. A town like Meridian, in other words, was a better place when there was a drugstore with a soda fountain downtown.

Aunt Nancy left Meridian and for many years ran a clothing store in Atlanta. She hates what the malls have done to the social experience of shopping. "You go to the mall, and you could be anywhere in the country," she said. "There's nothing distinct about it, and the service is horrendous. See, Sela, that's why people would go to the old downtowns. Here in Meridian there's Harry Mayer's, the quality men's store that's still downtown. His dad started that business years ago, and they always give great service. People long for that personal service you get from knowing who you're dealing with."

And for every holdout like Harry Mayer's, there are countless other Meridian institutions that are lying fallow. Take the old Opera House, for example. Back in the heyday of the railroad, I'm told, Meridian rivaled Birmingham and even Atlanta for sophistication. The city was prosperous, and cosmopolitan, enough to support a small opera house, which hosted performances by some of the greatest artists and entertainers of their time. The great Sarah Bernhardt sang there, and George Gershwin left his signature on his dressing room wall. You can still see it there today— but only if you're lucky enough to know someone who'll unlock the front door and let you in. Like so many others, the gorgeous, old-world jewel-box building now stands abandoned at the center of town.

Once we started returning to Meridian more often, I began thinking about ideas to help revive the old downtown of my childhood. Despite the weedlike spread of strip malls across America, after all, you can still visit neighborhoods in our older cities— Georgetown in Washington, the West Village and Brooklyn Heights in New York, Beacon Hill in Boston, among others—that retain (or have recaptured) that sense of thriving community space. It's hard to walk among the cobblestone streets and redbrick town houses of such places, their sidewalks and cafés bustling throughout the day, without swooning. There isn't a shopping mall on earth that's ever made me swoon.

So now I'm working with a handful of interested souls to raise money to restore the Opera House, hoping that a hint of revival in the downtown Meridian air might someday prove contagious. It's a dream of mine to help establish a performing-arts school behind that old brick façade, and I'm taking a real measure of care with it—

The Grand Opera House (left)

in part because of an unnerving experience I've had recently in connection with another Meridian landmark: Weidmann's.

Last year, when I learned that the owner of my favorite childhood restaurant was looking to sell, I went in with a group of interested locals to save the place. Our dream was to restore its kitchen
to its former glory as one of the most celebrated in the South, while
preserving the creaky charm of the interior space. But I'm learning a
sobering lesson in the process: once you've made the decision to
touch something old and dear with the magic wand of progress, you
can't always predict what's going to happen. Modern building codes
have already required more alterations in the interior than I'd have

liked, and food-service regulations are going to prevent the managers from returning those old homemade peanut-butter jars to their rightful place atop every table. I'm still excited about the new Weidmann's; when it opens up again late this year, I'm hoping its upgraded menu and first-class service will help bring people back downtown again. But inside I'll be waving a guilty goodbye to a little slice of my past.

It seems like ages ago now, but when I think of the best times Howard and I have had down South, my mind turns immediately to the summer of 2001. I remember the weekend as if time had preserved it in amber: the Mississippi heat suddenly turned less humid, the sweet scent of red earth lingering on the air.

The road from town out to our farm is framed with a canopy of gallant oaks; Howard and I drive past a cow pasture and an old white dairy barn; then it's one quick right turn and we're rolling up to the gates of the farm.

As we follow the little gravel drive that leads to the Rose Cottage, the sun shining lower now, I see up the road the figure of my towheaded son. Austin's going on eight, and his hair is growing longer in the back, like his father's. And somehow he's already talking a little like Howard, too—thoughtful and innocent, but with the glint of Howard's cleverness. I can't look at him without awe.

We slow down. "You want a ride?"

He smiles, through a mouthful of scrambled teeth. (If only there were an orthodontist in the family.) "No, I want to walk." He turns on his heel and sets off running, with a beckoning wave. "You follow."

He runs about a hundred yards, then flags, and steps over to the bank of our pond. We pull up alongside him again. He is transfixed by something sticking up out of the water. It's a broken old stump, one he's taken to calling the Turtle Camp. On the stump is a hand-sized creature, its head reaching out of its shell at the end of a long pencil neck. Austin's been spotting turtles for about a week now, and he can't get enough.

"It's the turtle, Mom." He's fixed it with a stare; I think he's wondering if it's the same one he's seen before. He's just had a good long sprint, but he's hardly winded. Then, just as he's trying to figure out whether he can coax the turtle to the shore with a stick, the little guy dives off the stump back into the water.

"Never mind," Austin says happily, and starts walking again. There'll be another one down the road.

Anabella is waiting when we arrive, with a gaggle of long-haired cousins and the rest of the family. Her cheeks are rosy with the afternoon's excitement. We give her hugs in turn.

"What are you wearing, honey?" She appears to be wearing both a dress and a little pair of pants. I seem to recall that being a fashion trend a few years ago among teenage girls, but I can't imagine it's trickled down to my four-year-old daughter.

"It's for the bugs," she answers. *Aha.* That's my husband's resourceful mind at work: long-sleeve dress to cover the arms, three-quarter-length pants to cover the legs. Plus—I pick up a whiff of it—a nice new spray of insect repellent. It's about five o'clock, and about this

time every day Howard worries that his daughter is going to become an all-you-can-eat Early Bird Special for the Mississippi mosquitoes. What amazes me is that Howard's been away all afternoon; apparently Anabella's learned to follow his lead.

The festivities are already under way at the cottage: drinks on the bank of the pond, beneath the weeping willows. The sun has gone down behind the trees, and the bullfrogs are chirping away at the prospect of dusk. The sweet smell of barbecue is in the air; the blades of the ceiling fans on the front porch spread the aroma like tangy sauce on white bread. Soon there'll be plates piled high with succulent beef ribs, chicken, snap beans, cornbread, and sweet-potato casserole.

It's my birthday.

We collect the kids and head on up to my brother Berry's place, where we'll gather with the rest of my family on his brick patio for a special performance. A men's barbershop chorus I've grown acquainted with has been kind enough to offer a miniconcert for me and my guests. They're rolling up the driveway in church vans just as we get there; we all shake hands, and they take their places at the edge of the patio, the sun setting over the fields, lighting them from behind.

It's still hot, and nobody would have begrudged the singers the mercy of shirtsleeves. But they all wore coats, ties, and church pants—all twenty or so. Southerners dress up as a matter of respect: respect for the occasion, for others, and for themselves. Those robust, red-cheeked fellows cut loose with some sweet old barbershop harmonies, but they really got the crowd going with a set of old-time gospel tunes like "When the Roll Is Called Up Yonder."

We stood and cheered after every number. "I just know y'all are Baptists!" yelped Becky, my pal from Birmingham. "Only Baptists can sing like that." The sound is exhilarating, and not least because these fellows are true gentlemen as well as artists. Their soft faces and kind eyes nearly make me cry. There's something so rare and beautiful about the face of a man who sings

> *Amazing grace, how sweet the sound*
> *That saved a wretch like me*
> *I once was lost, but now am found*
> *Was blind, but now I see*

. . . and means every word. There's no guile in these men's faces, and no pride—though their talent would earn them any pride they wanted to claim. I see only humility, warmth, and generosity.

Mama has come to hear them, too. Bill and Mark, two of the Birmingham Brigade, have taken places on either side of her, and they small talk with her between numbers. After the concert, those fine singers lean over to talk to her in her wheelchair. I sat on the steps watching this, just trying to imagine anything similar happening in L.A. No, I thought. But down here, out of common decency and respect for an elderly woman, these gentlemen keep my ailing mother company as I watch, quiet and warm.

That's a Southern man for you. After the chorus departs, we head back down to the cottage. My favorite cooks, Mr. and Mrs. Davis, bring out the barbecue spread, complete with hush puppies and spicy bread-and-butter pickles. We all pile our plates high, and retire to the long tables on the porch to eat, drink cold beer, and carry on.

Uncle Joe and Aunt Nancy are here. I listen quietly, never tiring of Uncle Joe's childhood stories; like Daddy's, they seem to come from a place and time impossibly out of reach. "There was a guy had a junk company right on the other side of the railroad track," he's saying. "We'd go down the railroad track, pick up a piece of scrap iron, put it in our wagon. And then, on our way downtown to go to the double feature, we'd go down to see that junkman, and he'd say, 'Oh, I'll give 'leven cents for it,' you know. Big old piece of iron, and all he'd give us was 'leven cents.

"So he'd take it and throw it in a pile back there, and we'd watch where he put it. Then after we went to the movies—it was just ten cents, you know, to get in the show—we'd come back at night and jump the fence, and steal that iron, and bring it back and sell it to him again. Get *twenty-two* cents out of it.

"And he thought he's messing *us* over, you know?"

When Uncle Joe chuckles, it comes from deep in his broad chest. Joe is a big, hearty man, over six feet tall, a baseball and football player in his prime, and still strong today at the age of seventy. I ask him about his grandfather, Grandaddy Joe Boswell, for whom he was named. "Didn't you say he was the only tall person in the family, before you?"

"Yeah," he says. "He came to our house one time. I must have been nine or ten. Rain, cold as hell, and everything. I went to open the door, and it was stormy and cold. And here's this big old guy, had on a damn black overcoat, and these damn black boots come up to his knees, and a big old black hat, and a gray beard. Look like something out of the movies, you see somebody like that, you know."

And he puts a low whiskey growl into his voice, recalling what that tall black-coated man said. "'Hey, there—*where's your daddy?*'"

He looks back at us. "Scared me to death."

As supper carries on, the Birmingham Brigade—Becky; her husband, Bill; her best friend Liz; and Liz's husband, Mark—keep us rolling with their tales of life among their social circuit back home. Liz was recently installed as president of the Birmingham Junior League, and Becky regales us with an account of the tribute Liz paid to her predecessor.

"It was wonderful!" Becky says. "I was all choked up. It was like Nixon's Checkers speech!"

Becky's exaggerating, of course—but among my hometown friends, you have to understand, exaggeration comes hand in hand with sincere praise. A Southern woman will carry on about a friend's marigolds as if they were the most exquisite blossoms on God's green earth.

I turn my head and catch a glimpse of Howard when he's not looking. He's always the sly spectator in these gatherings, hanging back and waiting for his moment to leap in with a clever jibe. He loves baiting Becky and Liz over questions of Southern manners and tradition. I don't know how it happens, but a few minutes later they start getting into it over the proper pan to use for pound cake.

"You make a pound cake in a Bundt pan," Becky is saying. "You don't make it in a loaf pan. That's what you *do!*" That last word gets stretched out to three syllables. "And you have monogrammed linens. I have that. My mother has that."

Poor Howard, bless his heart. I'm not sure he'll ever appreciate the difference between a Bundt cake and a loaf cake. But I think he's slowly absorbing the greater fact, which is that Southern life follows not the rules of logic, but the whims of poetry. The ways of Southern womanhood have always been distinct. After all, nobody's filming *Steel Magnolias* about the women of North Dakota, and a Ya-Ya Sisterhood has yet to be discovered in Rhode Island.

"I do think Southern women are caring," Liz offers. "You're caring to the point of never wanting your husband not to look good in a situation. You'll do all kinds of things to make sure nothing comes off wrong. And if another woman is getting ready to walk into a situation where she won't look good, you'll go out of your way to cover up for her, to avoid unpleasantries.

"But you have to be careful to look ahead, and anticipate these things, which is why it's so important to know all about people's history, and their families." She looks over at my husband. "Howard over there never talks about his family. I'll ask him, 'Now, Howard, who are your people? Where were you raised?' which is another way of asking, 'Who are you?' Nothing. With Sela, we know it all—all about her brothers and sisters, everything. When you go to New York or other places, people don't want you to know about them or their families. Down here, we're just dying to know. People are *fine* with their families, even if folks didn't turn out. You just say, 'Oh, he's going to turn out one day.'"

"Exactly!" says Becky. "If you don't have one or two characters in your family, you're hiding something big."

"My Aunt Gracie, she was a character," Liz says. "She would take to the bed for days. She was married forever, and during her whole marriage, she would never let her husband see her without makeup on. She would go to bed with it on, and get up early in the morning, greet her husband, then go into the bathroom, and not come out for hours. She'd be in there putting that makeup on."

She was a character—where I come from, that's a statement of pride. People in other parts of the country hide their eccentric relatives; Southerners put them on the front porch. And sometimes we put stranger things there, too. True story: A friend of mine had this uncle down in Louisiana, known to one and all as Big Guy. Big Guy won a tombstone off an unlucky undertaker in a poker game. He told the loser what he wanted as his epitaph, and had the final product delivered to the edge of his front porch. Every night for twenty years or so, Big Guy would go out and relieve himself before bedtime—on his own tombstone. It was his way of mocking death.

When Big Guy finally died, his children knew better than to second-guess his wishes. That's why today, if you visit Big Guy's grave, you can read his premeditated report on living conditions six feet under: THIS AIN'T BAD, ONCE YOU GET USED TO IT.

Wait—back up a minute, says one of the non-Southerners. What do you mean by "not turning out"?

"I can explain that," Becky says. "You know when you're cutting out cookies, and most of them turn out fine, but there's one that won't hold its shape? In a family, 'not turning out' means not living up to potential. If you come from humble circumstances, and you end up the manager of a truck-stop casino, then you turned out, for what you were raised to. But if you had a good mama and daddy, like Sela and Howard, but you still can't hold a job, or you're married five times, or you didn't marry right, then you didn't turn out."

But why are Southerners so concerned about family, anyway?

"If you know who somebody's family is, then you understand a lot about them," says Sam.

"It's the way we socialize," Becky agrees. "You'll meet a stranger in a social situation and ask her name and where she's from. It goes like this: 'A Calhoun from Jackson? My mama was sorority sisters with a Calhoun from Jackson. She married into the Memphis Simmonses—I'm related to them on my daddy's side.' And so forth."

I try to explain what it's like to be on the outside of their lifestyle, looking in. "Y'all have about fifty couples you're linked to," I say, "couples you socialize with in Birmingham. You have a history together, and you do things together, and you create a kind of comfort zone for yourselves." I tell them how much trouble we Hollywood types have developing social bonds, how the atmosphere's just a little too competitive. "You find yourself basing your social life on where you stand in the showbiz food chain. You don't really know who your friends are, and you can't always be sure you really have that many."

Liz knows what I mean; she's got friends on the West Coast. "Sometimes they go all weekend without seeing anybody they know," she says. "Honey, we can't go to the *mailbox* without seeing somebody we know. When somebody dies here, the first thing you do is take a casserole over. Even if it's somebody's aunt and you've never met her, you go, because you have to do the right thing."

Like I said, Howard knows how to spot an opening.

"You keep saying, 'Do the right thing, do the right thing.' " He grins. "But from what I hear, down here you've got more people sleeping around on their spouses than we do on the West Coast, where the rule isn't 'do the right thing' but 'do what works for you.' How is all that adultery 'doing the right thing'?"

Have you ever seen a porchful of people roll their eyes in unison? Howard has. We all call out together: "They're not doing the right thing!"

The point of all our customs and social rules, Becky reminds us, is to make sure everyone is taken care of—*despite* the transgressions we all know will occur. "Going to the funeral of somebody you don't care for, but who's a member of your family—well, you go out of respect to your family. Even if they did go crazy and shoot out all the plates; even if they had all kinds of scandalous affairs—good Lord, they're still your family. You *go*."

What Becky's getting at, I think, is captured in an old saying: *Hypocrisy is the tribute vice pays to virtue.* Just because Southerners find it hard to live up to high standards, in other words, doesn't mean those standards should be abandoned. If our standards are noble they should be aspired to, despite our human weaknesses. And this bedrock conviction, in turn, enables us to laugh at our hypocrisies, to make a joke of our failings. It's not a perfect way to live, but it seems to me to be the most tolerably human.

Liz has a ten-year-old daughter, and she and Becky get to trading stories about what it's like raising girls. "When something happens to your child," Liz says, "the littlest thing, like they don't get asked to spend the night when all the other girls are asked—it hurts you so badly. It breaks your heart."

"Do you remember this fall?" says Becky. "All the little girls were asked to spend the night at this party, except for my daughter. And I'm calling Liz from the car, and I'm like . . ." And she breaks down in a burlesque of sobbing. "I was ready to go over and have a *word* or two with that mother. Oh, God, do you remember that? We had to go over my mother's house. It was so bad, we had to go to Mama."

Liz smiles. "You had to have a Coke."

"And let me tell you—my mama started telling stories . . ." Becky continued.

". . . about when *I* had been left out . . ."

"She said, 'Oh, Lord, I remember when some little girl did that same thing once to you.' Now, I'd forgotten about it a month after it happened. But my mother was still *wounded*."

"And it's so funny about those kinds of things," Liz says, "because you can't tell your husband about them. 'Cause he's just not going to understand. So you call your friends. And whenever I call Becky and tell her something like that, she says, 'Now, what's that girl's name?'"

Becky knows her cue. "I say, 'I have *never liked* that girl, and she is *not* pretty.'"

We all guffaw.

"Liz will get over it, and I'll still be carrying a grudge. 'Just look at her,' I'll say. 'Legs like tree trunks!' We're loyal if nothin' else, I'll tell you that. . . ."

Once the plates have been cleared away, out comes the home-made ice cream. I step into the other room to check on the kids, and when I come back Becky's barreling into a story I know she's been saving all night.

"Y'all wouldn't believe how awful my feet were!" she says. "They had these thick rings of skin around 'em that looked like inner tubes. I sat there buck naked on the edge of my bathtub, going at 'em with a pumice stone. Lord, I worked myself into a sweat, and got nowhere.

"Then my precious angel of a husband came in and saw I was sweating. What a gentleman my darling is. He got right down on his knees and commenced to scrubbing. Do you all know that my nasty ol' feet wore that big strong man out?

"So I got dressed and went down to the hardware store. I went in there and asked the man, 'Do y'all have electric sanders?'

"He looked at me like I was a silly woman who didn't know what I was talking about, and he said, 'Do you want an orbital sander, or a regular one?'

"I told him, 'One that'll work on my feet.' He told me, 'I can't help you.' So I went myself and picked out one of those cute little mouse sanders they make.

"Well, I took it home, took my clothes off, and set myself up on the side of the bathtub. I got that sander to going, and *y'all!* It was like a snowstorm in there! Those inner tubes were just comin' to pieces, flyin' all over like a blizzard!"

The rest of us are doubled over by now, holding our sides. Finally one of us catches her breath enough to ask Becky how her feet came out.

"Oh, honey," she says. "They were like butter. Smooth as a baby's bottom. I'm a believer in that little ol' mouse sander. Now, Howard, you're a venture capitalist. What you need to do is get these things manufactured in pink and set me up on QVC, and I'll sell the hell out of these things. We'll just call it the Ped-o-file!"

And the laughter and stories carry us through to the end of the night.

Half to forget the wandering and the pain.
Half to remember the days that have gone by
And dream and dream that I am home again.

—James Elroy Flecker

8 ◎⟫

....

Now comes the hard part. I'm going to tell you about the worst season of my life. Yet, as painful and challenging as it was, in the end it was also a season of growth, of closure, and peace.

I look back on that wonderful gathering down on the farm, family and friends eating and drinking and laughing together, as if it were a picture postcard from another world. I could not have foreseen how long and bleak the winter that followed would be, nor how much I would despair that spring would come at all.

Days after returning to Los Angeles, I was sleeping late one morning when I felt Howard's hand on my shoulder, shaking me awake. His voice was tight in his throat. He said he'd just received a phone call from Sam, the contractor doing work on our house. "He was crying," Howard told me. "He said you won't believe it, but somebody flew two planes into the World Trade Center."

Was he serious? I was still coming out of sleep; none of this seemed real.

I scrambled out of bed and sat with my husband in front of the television, watching the world come to an end. We cried. We were in shock. We never left the TV. On some level we couldn't accept what we were seeing. It felt as if we were standing outside ourselves, watching this happen. I've since heard that many New Yorkers at first couldn't believe—literally could not believe—that someone had flown passenger planes into the Twin Towers. A friend stood on the Brooklyn Bridge, watching the towers burn, telling himself: *They won't fall*. Thirty seconds later the south tower collapsed, and my friend had to flee with an exodus of thousands to Brooklyn, just ahead of a cloud of dust and ash.

We may have been on the other side of the country that morning, but we didn't feel safe. Where would the terrorists strike next? We didn't let the kids go to school. I didn't want anyone leaving the house. We desperately wanted to go to the farm. I called my producers and said, "Look, if something major happens, we're headed to Mississippi." It's a very painful thing when you are trapped by things over which you have no control—as I was to learn again and again in the coming months.

I was angry that I didn't have the freedom to protect my kids. That day Austin asked me, "Mommy, are they going to hurt my school?" I said *no*—but I wasn't sure I believed it. Who could say for sure? There is a major shopping mall near his school, and as silly as it may seem now, on the morning of September 11 everything seemed like a target. I've talked to women from all over the country since then, and everyone, no matter how small and out-of-the-way their town was, felt just as vulnerable.

Then news reached us that Chic Burlingame, the brother of an old friend of our family, had been captain of the plane that was hijacked and crashed into the Pentagon. Investigators quickly concluded that the terrorists murdered the pilots of the airplanes before commandeering them. I called Chic's brother, Brad, to offer condolences, and he was sobbing on the phone. "They killed my brother. They killed my brother." Chic's birthday would have been September 12.

Of course, the authorities closed commercial airspace over the entire country in the immediate aftermath of the terror strikes. At night I would hear fighter jets flying overhead, and I'd think we were about to be attacked at any moment. I had nightmares about terrorists chasing me, or being on airplanes and having them narrowly miss a building. Howard and I tried to keep Austin and Anabella from seeing how frightened we were.

Now, you can allow yourself to be paralyzed by such fear, or you can learn from it, and act on what you've learned. Howard refused to be a passive victim. He went out to buy batteries, water, and other supplies we might need in case of a long emergency. No matter what happened, I knew that Howard would take care of us. I'm not ashamed to admit how desperately I needed to feel shielded, sheltered, and cared for during those days. Knowing my husband was there for us, come what may, helped me in turn to be strong and comforting to the kids.

Before the week was out, we began to hear talk of fund-raisers and charity events, but I was torn. I've always tried to be generous in this regard. But after 9/11 all I felt I could do, at least at first, was to stay close to my family, to be with Austin and Anabella. I didn't want to leave them, not for a minute more than was absolutely necessary. So many moms had kissed their children goodbye for the last time that morning, before going to work in the Twin Towers. I couldn't get out of my head a story I'd heard about one Brooklyn mom seen walking in a daze near the subway as the towers burned, telling passersby that she would have been there at her desk if her little boy hadn't made her late by crying so much about her leaving. You never know when that hug from little arms will be the last one you'll receive.

The one thing I did agree to was the September 21 telethon to raise money for the victims in New York and Washington. I'd felt so powerless, especially being so far away from New York, and I was glad for the chance to do something I knew would be meaningful. But I was scared, in part because the FBI had informed Hollywood executives that there'd been specific and credible threats against the studios that very morning. Howard and I left the kids at home with their nanny, and even as we were driving over to the studio he took my hand and wondered aloud if we were doing the right thing by going together. "What if something happens to us both? What about the kids?"

But we'd been assured that security for the event would be airtight, and we took from that enough comfort to continue. I've never heard a sound as reassuring as the whirring of helicopters circling overhead when we pulled up to the location.

The feeling on the set that night was low-key and friendly—as much so as I've ever experienced at a Hollywood event. Some, like George Clooney and Julia Roberts, were friendly faces I'd known and worked with before. Others were new acquaintances. I sat with Clint Eastwood; he'd been worried about his grandchild, who attended a school not far from the World Trade Center. We were all in the same position that day, humbled both by the magnitude of events and, I think, by the incredible courage and devotion we'd seen among the people of New York.

Those days were a time of great pain for us as a country, but they were days, too, when the meaning of our lives seemed suddenly clarified, amplified—more tangible, more real. They made me think of a story Walker Percy once told, the true account of a married couple on the Mississippi Gulf Coast who had been strangers to each other for years. When Hurricane Camille struck, they had to take refuge from the flooding in a tree house, of all things. As the eye passed overhead, they made love for the first time in years. The trauma of the storm shocked them out of their selfishness, and made them look at each other for the first time in ages. In the passing of the eye, they found that moment of revelation.

Maybe something like that happened to America on 9/11. People who donated blood, collected money, delivered food or aid or comfort of any kind to their fellow Americans rediscovered a lost sense of neighborliness, of human kindness—the virtues that made America home. As Becky might have said, everyone did the right thing.

Can we still? Can we carry the love and pride and self-sacrifice that got us through the tough times with us now that life is getting back to where it used to be, more or less? I suppose it's a challenge we face as a country: how to be as decent to each other in good times as we were in the depths of crisis. As Rabbi Heschel said, "Our concern is not how to worship in the catacombs but rather how to remain human in the skyscrapers."

When November rolled around, Howard and I knew one thing instinctively: The Sherman family was going to spend this Thanksgiving together in Los Angeles, close by one another in our own home. It wasn't an easy decision; it meant we wouldn't make it to Mississippi, and I knew that would disappoint Mama as much as it did me. I think we were all sad not to be able to celebrate as we had so often in the past, with all the generations gathered together at one table. But the truth is, I was scared to death to put my family on an airplane so soon. And there was another thing: It had begun to dawn on me that my kids didn't really know what it was like to celebrate a holiday in their own home. *Maybe it's time they learned,* I thought.

In January, just as life finally seemed to be getting somewhat back to normal, I began to realize that I'd soon be facing another change in my life. For three years I'd been playing the role of a lifetime as an actress—and now it looked as though that wonderful gift was about to be withdrawn.

After *Sisters* ended its six-year run in the late 1990s, I came out of that show knowing I had earned my chops, and certain I would still be in the running for starring film roles. Wrong. One of the first things I did post-*Sisters* was audition for a femme fatale role in the James Bond movie *Tomorrow Never Dies.* I thought things went terrifically well with the director. Then my manager called to give me the news.

"Sela, I don't know how to tell you this," he said, "but the director told me, 'What I really want is Sela Ward ten years ago.'"

I was thirty-nine. I'd never felt more sexy and more confident as a woman, and more ready as an actress. Yet as I quickly discovered, if you were over thirty-five, you weren't any of those things as far as Hollywood is concerned. Once again, I was being told that the only thing that mattered was my looks. Crushed, I went up to Santa Barbara on retreat to nurse my wounded ego. As I sat soaking in a bathtub, reading an article on why women lie about their age after thirty-five, I came across the story of a postmenopausal woman in the Midwest, who still kept tampons in her desk so people would think she was younger. It was an awful story, but I thought: *Thank God—I'm not the only one worrying about my age.*

Just as I reached the age of forty—and just as I was becoming convinced that my Hollywood career might be losing steam, I was handed the best-written TV script I'd ever read. It was for a new show called *Once & Again,* and one of its lead roles was a character named Lily Sammler, a divorced forty-year-old mother of two daughters taking a second chance at love. As much as I didn't want to go back to doing an hourlong television series, *Once & Again* had me from the first page of the pilot script. I knew Lily, I adored Lily, and at some level, I *was* Lily. Happily, Ed Zwick and Marshall Herskovitz, the show's creators, agreed, and cast me in the role.

We debuted in the fall of 1999. The critics loved us. Unfortunately, not enough viewers did. ABC moved the show around on its schedule constantly, hoping to find an audience, but by the middle of the third season it became obvious that the ratings were never going to be what we'd all hoped. By the spring of 2002, there were whispers on the set that the show was in serious trouble.

Truth to tell, I had mixed feelings about the show coming to an end. I loved Lily more than any other character I'd played. As exhilarating as my work on *Sisters* had been, I had never given myself so wholly to the art of acting until I began work on *Once & Again*. But the ongoing concern about ratings was draining, a constant distraction: here I was, sure that I was doing the best acting of my career, and all the while I knew I was about to lose this wonderful role, this intelligently written and deeply felt character, because not enough people were tuning in to keep it going.

And there was another consideration. In those three years I gave so much creative effort on-screen (and on the set) to this new family, this group of writers and directors and producers and fellow actors who all pulled together to tell this story every week. I had tapped into a real flow of positive energy, and given my all to the cast and crew I considered my second family.

But at the same time I knew all along, every early morning when I left for work and every late night I came home, that all that energy might have gone elsewhere—not to Lily Sammler's family, but to my own. I worried about that. And in my heart I wanted it to be over.

Then, at the end of January, I picked up the phone and there was Jenna's voice. She was sobbing.

"Sela, Mama's really sick," she said. "She's in the hospital, and she didn't feel like talking on the phone. You know how she *always* wants to talk. Daddy told me, 'Jenna, she's fighting hard, but this is too much. I don't think she's going to make it.' Sela, he started crying." Our daddy doesn't cry.

We'd been through this before. Mama had been seriously ill for nine years or so, and had cheated death more times than I care to recall, usually with all of the kids at her side. But no matter how sick Mama had been in the past, Daddy always insisted she was going to pull through. This time was different.

The producers were gracious enough to charter us a plane, even rearranging my shooting schedule to allow me till Sunday to be with Mama. I gathered up my brother Brock, who also lives in L.A., and together we headed home, arriving in Meridian at four o'clock the next morning.

When we reached Mama's bedside, it was obvious that she was in a lot of pain. Her lungs were failing. She'd had lung episodes in the past, but after a brief hospital stay for treatment she usually felt good enough that she'd be back in action a couple days later. Not this time. The steroids the doctors gave her had made her bones brittle, and they were beginning to fracture, causing her frightful pain. The lung specialist had talked with Daddy and Jenna outside Mama's room the night before. She had about a month to live, he told them, and the doctors needed to know whether we wanted Mama revived if her lungs should give out.

Jenna filled me in. "If we wanted her to be revived, he said, they could do it. But it would be rough, and probably break some of her bones. I told him I didn't want her to go through that. He said he'd make sure everyone knew that."

Brock, Jenna, Daddy, and I took turns sitting with Mama. Berry had his hands full at work, and couldn't spend as much time with her as he might have wanted; but then, as her one child who'd stayed behind in Mississippi, he'd always been there for her. I think he was relieved that his three siblings had come to help him shoulder the burden.

Those next few days were difficult. There was a constant parade of family and friends through Mama's hospital room, and it was unnerving to watch as she smoked (yes) and held court, pretending she wasn't going to die. Some days she'd be laughing so uproariously you'd look at her and think, *She's going to be fine*. But the truth was, she knew as clear as day what was happening, and we knew just as surely that she couldn't handle it. It was frightening enough for us to confront the thought that this was the end. But the vision of our headstrong Mama refusing to acknowledge the fact that she was going to die, was almost too much to bear.

We called everyone who was close to Mama—her brother in Tennessee; her best friend, Betty; her niece in Jackson and her kids; my aunt in Birmingham and her daughter—and told them that this was it, that they needed to come say goodbye.

Jenna decided to call Tom Sikes, a new minister at First Christian Church, and ask his advice. We'd never met this new pastor before, but all we knew to do was reach out in Mama's time of need. Mama was very sick, Jenna told him; she needed to talk with someone about dying, but it wasn't going to be any of us. Maybe he could come around and see if he could help.

Later that day my sister brought Daddy home from the hospital, and when she returned to Mama's room the handsome young pastor stood up to greet her. "Hi. I'm talking to your mother about death," Tom said.

"Okay. Well, I'll just go get a Coke and come right back," Jenna said.

By the time she returned Mama and Tom were laughing and joking, just as she always did. He stayed about an hour. When Jenna showed him out, he took her into the hallway.

"Your mama said, 'I'm going to walk the road I'm on, and I'm going to need your help,'" he told her. At last a concession; at last a request for support. We all breathed a sigh of relief.

Mama could never have told us kids directly what she was going through. She had spent too many years trying to protect us. But Tom Sikes was there for just that reason. He'd lost his own family, I learned later; he'd addressed death firsthand, and he knew what language to use.

One night, as Mama lay dying, Jenna and I had an intimate talk with Daddy. He told us why certain things had happened the way they had in the life of our family—things he and Mama had endured but kept from us children, for our own peace of mind. They had suffered for each other and from each other, he told us, but they had endured. At last he could no longer keep up his façade; he wept not just for Mama, but for his cousin James who died in the war, for his Aunt Margaret, and for years of unreleased tears. It was a moment of mercy, and we all wept with thanks.

At last Mama's family started arriving; though not one of us said so, we all knew the time was coming near. Jenna kept a diary of Mama's last days, and she recorded the aunts' and cousins' visits faithfully. "When I saw all her relatives coming," she wrote, "I just further understood that everything is in order. She is saying goodbye. Dear Lord, I need not worry, I know you are doing everything and I appreciate the beauty of all of this, as I find it so hard."

Sitting by our mother's bedside, Jenna also wrote: "Oh little, little one. You are so tiny. You are so sweet. So courageous. So strong. I wish you didn't have to be so strong. I wish you could just be taken care of. I wish your lungs were strong again. I wish I could have been closer . . . maybe your friend. I pray that your lungs will quietly take you away and that cancer doesn't ravage your body to the end. I guess you're blessed that the cancer will not eat you away. But what is it like to drown in your own lungs? Peaceful, I hope. I wish you would sleep. Thank you, Mama, for everything. I am grateful. There is so much grace. There is so much grace."

That night, Jenna and I huddled on either side of the bed in Mama's room, talking and laughing with her on into the deep of night. Mama stopped at one point, looked at us, and said, "Isn't this fun, just the three of us here together?" It was as if we were all hunkered down at the farm, telling stories in the middle of a winter storm. At one point, Mama's mood seemed light enough that Jenna felt able to take a chance. So she turned to Mama, and told her she could leave us whenever she felt ready. "You mean kick the bucket?" Mama laughed sassily, all Bette Davis–like.

The next day, after breakfast, I was due to return to L.A. to resume filming. Leaving my mother's bedside after four emotionally charged days was one of the most painful things I've ever had to do. I took her face in my hands, savored her sweet smell, and told her, "I'll be back, Mama. I promise."

"I know you will," she whispered. "I know you will."

That made one of us. On Monday morning I showed up back at work, determined to find it within me to remain professional despite the state of my heart. But I was haunted by my promise. *What if I don't get back before she dies? What if she dies this week, while we're filming?* Mama had to hang on until the weekend. I so needed to be with her as she breathed her last breath. I was in a horrible position.

But what could I do? The *Once & Again* producers had been marvelous in accommodating my needs for time off during my mother's last days. They had generously chartered the first plane home, and spent several days shooting scenes around my character. They had done everything they could for me, but now they were hard up against the reality that nothing more could be done on the program without me. Had I stayed in Mississippi past the weekend, production would have had to shut down at the cost of $80,000 a day. I would just have to deal with the guilt, and pray to God for just a few more days of life for Mama.

I pushed myself through those days, nerves frayed, exhausted and distracted. I stayed in constant touch with Jenna, and she told me Mama was getting weaker and weaker. I would go to my trailer to cry. I prayed: "God, please help me. I don't know what to do." I needed to be there at the end, but nobody could say when that would be—days or weeks or longer. She had come back from the brink so many times before.

It was the worst week of my life. I was tempted to walk off the set, and leave everyone holding the bag. But I talked myself off that ledge, convinced that it would have been wrong to do that to the others. Still, what about my obligation to Mama? I was enraged that at such an important moment in my life I wasn't free to do what I wanted to do. The helplessness I'd felt in the wake of September 11 came back a thousandfold, and was compounded by the guilt I felt—the simple guilt of surviving a loved one's death.

I'd get a knock on my trailer door. "You're needed on the set,

Miss Ward!" a young man would shout. I'd pull myself together, run to makeup, and become Lily Sammler. For the most part—save for a tearful moment on the set's staircase—I found myself able to lose myself as I spoke Lily's lines, living her problems, so focused on her that there was no room for other thoughts. In times of crisis, work can be a great painkiller.

The cast and crew stood by my side, and held me up when I couldn't do it alone. Marin Hinkle, who played my TV sister Judy, was particularly kind and loving. My director, Dan Lerner, and costar Billy Campbell couldn't have been gentler or more patient. The most moving moment for me came when one of the grips whispered to me, "You want us to call in sick with the blue flu?" He was offering to organize the crew into a sickout, allowing me to return home. His offer brought tears to my eyes. I thanked him, but begged him not to do it. And so he didn't. What made all their concern even more poignant was the fact that we were anxiously awaiting word from the network about whether the show would be renewed for another season. At any moment, we could all be told we were out of a job.

Normally I would have found much solace in the arms of my children, but I rarely saw them. I'd leave for the *Once & Again* set in Culver City before they were awake, and wouldn't get home until they were in bed asleep. I talked to them on the phone every day, and brought them to the set a couple of times, but it wasn't nearly enough.

Thank God for Howard. No matter how early I got up in the morning, or how late I arrived home, he was always awake for me, ready to put his arms around me and let me cry. Howard was on the phone with Mama daily, trying to lift her spirits. He even tried bribing her, offering $100 a day in casino money if she'd only stop smoking and start eating. He told her she could use the money to play the slot machines, a late-in-life obsession that Howard felt sure was almost as strong as her addiction to tobacco. When she heard his offer, she just chuckled, "Sure." Then lit up another cigarette.

Mama became a serious slot-machine fan when the Silver Star Casino opened a few years ago in Philadelphia, Mississippi. Vicki Savoy, who handled VIP arrangements for the casino, was fond of Mama, and always looked after her for me. Every now and then Mama would take Vicki up on her offer to send a car to pick her up, but she wouldn't let it pull into her driveway. She was afraid the Baptist neighbors would see the Silver Star logo on the door and disapprove, so she had the driver meet her down the road, at a convenience store. But more often Desiree Jennings, her caregiver, would drive her up to the casino when she felt good enough to play the slots. We knew it was her escape from the realities of her cancer, and I was so thankful that she had something to look forward to.

So there I was, stuck in L.A., agonizing over my mother's failing health, waiting for my show to die, working eighteen-hour days, never seeing my children, who had to face the fact that their grandmother was about to die, and their mom wasn't there to help them through it. People tell me I'm an optimist, but I have never despaired as I did that week. I wanted to run home: home to Mama, home to Meridian, home to a time and place that seemed so simple, innocent, and loving, at least in my memory.

So I white-knuckled it through that week, waiting for a phone call that mercifully never came. I finished filming at three in the morning on a Friday, climbed aboard a charter flight the next morning, and landed in Meridian that afternoon. I went straight to the hospital, and never left until it was over.

Mama was so brave. One night early in that week, she could have died if she had just let herself go. Brock was sitting up with her, holding her up as she struggled to breathe. She said, "I wish . . . I just wish there was a pill I could take to end this."

Brock told her he might be able to find something.

But apparently she thought twice. "No," she said. "When it's my time, God will take me." And then she made it through the night. After this, Jenna told me later, she knew Mama wouldn't allow herself to go until I got back home. She was waiting for me.

The hospital gave us a guest room for the night; we slept there in shifts, when we weren't keeping Mama company. She had by then become so weak she couldn't lift her legs by herself. She was still awake and alert, but a film had descended over her eyes. Her fragile ribs were starting to crack, and the fluid in her lungs was suffocating her. She was given morphine to help her relax, to help dampen the sheer panic that comes with losing the use of your lungs. She'd beg us not to leave her; her greatest fear was dying alone. "Mama," we would reassure her, "Mama, we're not leaving you."

Her own strength was ebbing, and yet she could still demand it from us. At one point, one of us began weeping by her bedside. Mama lifted one stern finger. *"Not in my house!"*

As her life drained away, though, a childlike spirit seemed to come over her. On the night when she nearly died in Brock's arms, he heard her say, "I love you, too, Mama." She talked about seeing birds flying outside her window, even when there were none to be seen; we wondered if the morphine was making her hallucinate, but somehow we thought not. And she began singing eerie little rhymes, nonsense songs that none of us had ever heard:

Wrap it all up, roll it in a ball,
roll it down the hall,
See you on the other side!

Later, to no one in particular, she said the word "Gabriel," and gave a little chuckle. Jenna told us that she had quietly been praying to the Archangel Gabriel to come help Mama, and that a spiritual friend of Jenna's had phoned to say she had a feeling the archangel was present in Mama's room. Jenna had never mentioned this to anyone, and you never heard Mama talk about Biblical characters, ever. I wonder whether, through the drug-induced haze, she had found some way to peer through the curtain to the other side.

Finally, during one of those endless days, I was alone in the room when a doctor came by and asked me into the hallway. He told me her lungs were filling up again.

"If this were your mama," I asked him, "what would you do?"

Bless that man for being honest with me. She wasn't going to get any better, he told me. "Aside from her lungs, her cancer's inoperable. She's really weak, and if she were my mama, I wouldn't put her through any more aggressive procedures," he said. "They just won't have a positive result." He told me that if we wanted to do the merciful thing, we could bring her suffering to an end by easing off her life-support regimen and simply allowing her body to shut down.

"We can keep her comfortable," he said. "It'll take no more than forty-eight hours."

I couldn't make this decision alone. I called Jenna over at Mama and Daddy's house, and we got Daddy on the phone. He said that Mama wouldn't want to be placed on a ventilator, and we all knew that was true. The decision had to be made. We made it, and I let the doctors know.

I felt as if I had just given the order to kill my mother.

I made it down to the nurses' station and called Jenna, begging her to come be with me. I started sobbing uncontrollably. The nurses, those sweet, sweet ladies, came over and held my hand and comforted me.

And then the whole family arrived. Jenna, Berry, Brock, Daddy, and me. We gathered around Mama, and Berry began to speak to her. His tears came before his words did. He said, "Mama, I want you to know we're all going to be okay, that we'll take care of each other." She had been our rock, our touchstone, our protector, and our friend; Berry's tears were for us as well as for her.

We had spent the last nine years trying to keep Mama alive, through cancer, emphysema, and other illnesses. Whenever she took ill, all four of us would rush to her side, confident that our love would somehow carry her through. Once, when she was in the hospital for an aortic aneurysm operation, she stayed forty-five days, and we were right there with her; after she pulled through, surprising even the doctors, we Ward siblings were left with an illusion of omnipotence, a feeling that we had the power to keep her alive, if only we could be with her and love her hard enough.

In the end, the most loving thing we could do was to let her go.

We watched her breathing grow shallower and shallower over the next twenty-four hours. Pastor Sikes was summoned, as were her closest relatives. Tom suggested that we stand around Mama together and start sharing happy memories, even telling funny stories about our lives together. That Tuesday morning, the doctors told us she probably wouldn't make it through the day. Mama was gasping for air; her head was arched back, mouth open, desperate to breathe. Her eyes were shut and her neck was rigid.

We called everybody and told them Mama had only a couple of hours left. All the aunts, uncles, and cousins rushed down. Even Desiree Jennings, who had been Mama's caregiver and friend during her final years, came and never left until the end. We surrounded her bed, and each person touched a part of her body. Daddy held one hand, her brother had the other; Aunt Sarah caressed one of Mama's feet, Berry had a hand on one leg, and Brock on the other. I had my cheek resting on Mama's forehead, and Jenna was next to me on Mama's right side. We cradled her, and caressed her, and told her again and again that it was all right to let go. With each passing moment, she slipped further and further from our grasp.

There was, in those long moments, a wonderful warmth in the air, the kind of easy feeling Mama always created around her. The streak of irreverence in our family was there, too; when Tom recited a psalm that didn't seem to fit the moment, we told him, "No, we don't like that one. Read the last one again." And between readings we would take turns sharing memories from our lives with Mama. "We love you, Mama, we love you," we murmured. "We love you."

And then she took her final labored breath with those exhausted

With Mama in 1998.

lungs, and she died. A tear dropped down her cheek. Mama, unsentimental to the last, was finally able to cry.

"Look up and blow her kisses," Tom said. All of us raised our tear-streaked faces, kissed the palms of our hands, and waved goodbye to Mama. Then we joined hands, standing in a circle around her, and sang "Amazing Grace."

That is how Annie Kate Ward, my mother, left this world.

The day before she died, we kids left the hospital and went to the farm to find a suitable place to bury her. We had never discussed it with her; she was so conscious about spending money, and we knew just what she'd say: "I already have a plot paid for, out there where my parents are buried." But it was a run-down cemetery on the outskirts of town, and we weren't going to leave our mama there. So we made the proper arrangements with local authorities, and set out to find her a place on our own land.

The four of us went with Daddy to the lower part of the farm, below the railroad track. At first we thought of burying Mama in the pecan grove there, because she was so fond of those pecan trees. But I remembered her saying in the hospital how lonely the sound of a train is, and I decided I couldn't have her hearing that whistle every day. So we found a spot on a hill behind the Rose Cottage, within view of all three lakes, where she could be closer to where the rest of us lived. Mama's grave would begin the family cemetery.

The afternoon she died, after they'd taken Mama's body away, Brock said, "I'm going to dig her grave." He began to dig on the hill, and after darkness fell, came in and asked for an electric lantern. The next morning Berry helped him finish, and Jenna and I even got down into the hole to help out.

"Look at this," Brock said. Two feet down, he showed us the remains of an old campfire. It had to have been kindled by Indians; there are lots of arrowheads along the creek that runs through the farm. With Jenna sitting at the foot of the grave writing in her journal, I stood below her in the bottom of the hole, shovel in hand. I breathed in deep the rich, heady aroma of that Mississippi earth. My Mississippi earth.

On Wednesday afternoon we held a private family viewing at the funeral home, before the casket was closed for good. The four of us kids were there, but Daddy didn't want to come. He didn't want to see her like that. But she looked so much better there, at rest, than she had at the end of her struggle in the hospital, and I found myself wishing he'd come to see her, so that his last memory of her face would be one of serenity and beauty.

Still, when I arrived I saw at once that one thing was missing. And so, before I would let anyone else approach the casket, I pulled out Mama's favorite Revlon Love That Red and did her lips one last time. She would never have let anyone see her without it and there was no reason this should be any different. Now, with red roses in her hands to match her lipstick, Mama was ready.

Then my dear assistant, Jackie, drove up, came in quietly, and told us that Daddy was on his way in from the car. He walked in behind her, joined his children, and we all stood there holding each other, praying for her one by one, and took our turns saying goodbye.

That night we had visitation at the church. We arranged a centerpiece of framed photos of Mama at stages throughout her life, surrounded by candles. She had always hated dreary funeral music, so we had her favorites, Glenn Miller and Tommy Dorsey, playing. For two hours people filed by in the receiving line to pay their respects. At one point, I looked up and the director of Hope Village had come by with the six orphan girls from the Village. Two of them broke down in sobs. I remember holding one and saying, "It's okay, honey, it's okay. We're going to take care of you. You're safe."

"Death in a small town is a different proposition from death in a large city," writes Willie Morris. "Death in a small town deeply affected the whole community. For weeks or even years the physical presence of the dead person would be missed in specific places; his funeral itself would touch closely upon the life of the town."

It seemed as though the whole town turned out to pay its respects, either at the visitation or at the funeral the next day. This is how it is in a small town: in a place where families lead their entire lives in close proximity, simple shared history is enough to bring people together in times of need. "Ask not for whom the bell tolls/It tolls for thee"— John Donne's words are felt keenly by small-town people, who cannot pretend not to notice when someone has passed away.

In the days immediately surrounding my mother's death, I really saw that we were not alone in the world. People who were more or less strangers to us came out to help because we were their neighbors, and we were part of the town. That's all. As I was getting into the car to leave the funeral for the burial, I saw the mother of a high school friend run over to me. She had lost a daughter my age to cancer. She looked at me through the car window, and said, "Sela, I'm just so sorry." She went out of her way to connect, to let me know she shared my suffering. That I was not alone.

Not long ago, I heard Tom preach a sermon on why you should go to church. Besides worshiping God, he said, you should go because it is there that you'll find people who love you. He ended up preaching four funerals that month—and I know he and the congregation ministered to those grieving families every bit as well as they ministered to mine.

He eulogized Mama well at her funeral. "She fought the good fight," he said. God was there to receive her, to help her overcome disease and despair. He would offer her a new body, a new set of lungs. "And she is dancing in heaven as we gather!"

Only family and close friends were invited to the graveside service. We followed the hearse down the gravel road, through the gate to the farm, and down the hill, past the picnic tree, around the lakes, and finally up that last hill behind the Rose Cottage. We had arranged for a gospel choir to sing at the burial. Mama would have hated it; she despised anything remotely sentimental. The choir was for the rest of us. And I know the sight and sound of that group, their white robes with green collars flowing out behind them, their faces open with welcome as we arrived, brought comfort to us all.

I had one of my favorite poems, by Henry van Dyke, read aloud for Mama:

> *I am standing upon the seashore.*
> *A ship at my side spreads her white sails to the morning breeze*
> *and starts for the blue ocean.*
> *She is an object of beauty and strength.*
> *I stand and watch her until at length*
> *she hangs like a speck of white cloud just where the sea*
> *and sky come to mingle with each other.*
> *Then someone at my side says*
>
> *"There she is gone!"*
> *"Gone where?"*
> *Gone from my sight. That is all.*
> *She is just as large in mast and hull and spar*
> *as she was when she left my side and she is just*
> *as able to bear her load of living freight to her destined port.*
> *Her diminished size is in me and not in her.*
>
> *And just at the moment when someone at my side says,*
> *"There she is gone!"*

There are other eyes watching her coming,
And other voices take up the glad shout
"Here she comes!"
And that is dying.

Tom mentioned the breeze, and the beautiful day. He told us about the Resurrection, and why it was good to sing in a cemetery. Brock and I had elected to offer some final words. When it was his turn, Brock had one hand on the casket, and the other on his heart. He wept as he talked about how much he loved Mama. Yet it was not somber on top of that hill. I knew, just knew, that Mama would be ticked if we all sat there helplessly wailing. I stood up and said, "You all know Mama would be furious at us for standing around crying. We need to all think of her hitting the jackpot in heaven's casino, of being able to dance again because her legs are healed." Something came over me, I found the right words to say, and I felt the joy in my heart coming forth. After we had taken our turns speaking, we watched as our mother was lowered into the ground, and shared the task of shoveling the sweet-smelling soil onto her casket. And then we left.

I took Howard's hand, and walked with him down the hill to gather the kids. I was so tired and emptied out I didn't know what to say. We drove up together to Berry's house to eat and visit with friends and mourners. When we arrived, I couldn't believe my eyes.

Berry's friends had come in droves and set up tables laden with food. They had decided that we didn't have enough, so they went out and bought some more. Some other pals of his showed up with aprons on, and started barbecuing. They just took over, because they knew we wouldn't have the strength to. Some of them weren't particularly close friends, just folks who had grown up in our neighborhood. Once a neighbor in this small town, always a neighbor. Becky and Liz drove over from Birmingham to offer support. My college roommates Ginger and Connie drove in from Alabama. My girlfriend Martee even flew in, all the way from Philadelphia, because she thought I needed to know how much she loved me. And our pastor, Tom Sikes, was a bridge across a stormy canal that none of us could have crossed unguided.

I have never been more in touch with true love than in those days, and I shall never forget it. In those weeks before and after Mama's death, I discovered anew the miraculous strength of my friends—no matter where they lived. Whether they were there for us in Meridian—like Manny and Melanie, Jeanne and Sally—or in Los Angeles, like Ann and Ron, Carrie and Pam—they offered good, strong shoulders and welcome advice in equal measure. And my assistant, Jackie, who seemed to love my mother as if she were her own, put much of her own life on hold to keep me going through it all. In a time when America was discovering its own heroes in the wake of September 11, I found myself blessed with heroes of my own.

Weeks later, Jenna and I were talking, and I mentioned how much it meant to me for Aunt Nancy to hold me tight in the hospital as I fell apart. Jenna nodded.

"I'll always remember the day before Mama died," Jenna said, tears brimming. "Walking into her room, and watching Aunt Celeste holding Mama's hand as she said, 'Help me, help me.' Sela, they were all there. It wasn't just us. We lost Mama, but look what we gained."

Woodman, spare that tree!
Touch not a single bough!
In youth it sheltered me,
And I'll protect it now.

—George Pope Morris

9 ☽

If I'd been able, I would have stayed in Mississippi for weeks after Mama died. But I had a show to do. We buried Mama on Valentine's Day, a Thursday, and I had to be on the set ready for work Tuesday morning, five days after I cradled my mother's head in my arms for the last time.

Friends of mine would later tell me they're astonished that I managed to finish the last episodes of *Once & Again* with my wits about me. My grief for Mama was still raw. The cast was waiting any day for the network to axe us. And to make matters worse, in these final episodes Lily, my character, was losing her mother to Alzheimer's disease, and trying to figure out how to say goodbye. I have no idea how I made it through those scenes; my memory of those last weeks is a blur. I once read that the emotion of grief can exact a real physical toll on a body, racking it with fatigue and exhaustion, and now I know that to be true. On my first day back, I had to grab hold of a washer and dryer on the set and hold on to it to keep from collapsing. Eventually my nerves simply got the better of me, and collapse I did.

The official word came down on March 28: the series would be history by mid-April. I was too worn out to be sad. There was a time when I would have thought having your show yanked out from under you was pretty much the end of the world. Watching your mother die puts things in perspective.

After we filmed the final episode, I said goodbye to my dear friends in the cast and left town. I needed to think about everything that had happened: The end of my time on *Once & Again*. Those images we'd seen over and over on television, of the people of New York running for their lives or mourning their loved ones. That image of my own mother, taking her last breath, despite all her children's efforts to keep her alive.

I reflected back upon those moments, and I thought, *We all could be dead in the twinkling of an eye.*

Just as they had after Austin was born, questions flooded my mind during this difficult season—questions that seemed at once irrational and deadly important. *Who would look after Daddy if I were to die? After my siblings and their families? Who would keep my children safe? Who would look after Howard?* I was struggling to find a safe place, to find clarity, to find relief from this crippling anxiety.

At long last, I realized: the key to it all was Mama.

After I started my own family, when I began looking southward again and thinking about writing this book, I thought it was a simple urge I was following—to come home again, to regain contact with a simpler way of life, to foster a real connection between my young children and my older, wiser parents.

Then Mama passed away, and for a moment the world she left behind felt impossible to sustain. My creative outlet was gone. The survival of my family was under threat. My Daddy was on his own. And I had lost my rock of comfort and support.

Only then did it begin to come into focus, just what a deep and complex legacy Mama had left for me. There was nothing simple about it.

It's one of the hardest things we can do, to come to know our parents. We grow up watching them through the wrong end of a telescope; we think we're watching all there is to see of them, but the image we see is limited, finite, and heartbreakingly remote. We can never know them the way they were as children, for instance, or as courting lovers. We never know just exactly what went on after we were sleeping at night; we can only assume that they argued about money or family, and hope that now and then they slipped outside to kiss on the porch.

But if we're lucky, we have friends and relatives who find the right time to show us the view through their telescopes. They share their memories, and when they do—again, if we're lucky—a new, more three-dimensional picture can begin to emerge.

I have my own store of memories of Mama. Most of what I've told about here comes from among them. But there's more to tell, and much of it may be—for me, anyway—far more important.

First of all, she was a gifted woman, possessed of intelligence, keen perception, unshakable character, and an appetite for hard work. But Annie Kate lived in a time and place that gave her few

options for self-fulfillment. She grew up poor and I think secretly ashamed of it, married and had four children in almost as many years. And she learned early how to steel herself against life's disappointments. I think now of what her childhood must have been like—those Depression times Uncle Joe recalls so vividly—and I realize she must have been like a flowering plant in rocky soil, that could survive but never bloom.

In Daddy, Mama married a man who was handsome and strong, and a good provider. But he was difficult, too—demanding and not always able to give in return. Still, she loved him, and was committed to him and to the children they had together. These were the cards she was dealt in life, and she did with them what she could.

Though I wasn't aware of it when I was a child, I think that many of the people around her recognized the sacrifices my mother made in raising us. She made a kind of faith out of denying herself, as if even a well-deserved pleasure were a sinful indulgence. Once, I remember—I was maybe nine or ten years old—we all went with Daddy to buy Mama a beautiful mink stole as a gift. She knew the joy it gave him to buy it for her, and I know that on some level she loved having it. But in the end my mama just couldn't allow herself something like that. She took it back to the store as soon as the moment had passed.

And they weren't strictly sacrifices of disposable income or creature comfort that she avoided. When I was young, my mother helped my father keep the books for his engineering office. Aunt Nancy remembers her as a woman whose potential was obvious, but underutilized. "She only had a high school education," Nancy says, "but she was very shrewd in business. This was before computers; everything was written longhand. She mastered it all. And nothing got by her—did she *ever* know who owed what, when, and where! If she'd had the opportunity she could have run a Fortune 500 company."

Later, though, as computers entered the workplace, Nancy watched as the march of technology seemed to outpace Mama's self-assurance. "She didn't believe in herself enough, didn't have a lot of confidence in her abilities. With any kind of schooling, education—if at some stage in her life someone had taken the time to talk her through these new machines, had showed her what she was intimidated by, she could have mastered anything. But by that time all she'd say was, 'I can't learn all this, Nancy. I'm too old.'" (It was the same refrain when we urged her to cut out the cigarettes that would eventually kill her: "I'm too old to quit.")

And so Mama stuck to what she knew. She worked, and worried, and developed a kind of defensive shell around herself that wasn't always easy to penetrate. She always refused to pity herself, which is why she hated sentimentality: if she had started down that road, she might not have been able to find her way back. Besides, self-pity is a sign of weakness, and she had passed her whole life fighting to stave off weakness.

Mama protected us, and gave us all her native strength. But here is the hardest truth: It wasn't given to her to *nurture* us, to help us recognize our dreams and chase them. As much as she took care of her children, sheltered us, and provided for us, she'd never been given the tools young people need to foster their own potential, and so she was unable to pass them on to us. She never knew how to set us on the right path, only how to guard and hold us close. And I have lived my life running from, and returning to, her all-encompassing embrace.

As Mama's eldest daughter, I see now that much of her repressed longing and ambition was displaced onto me. And in turn I came to fulfill a certain unstated role in the family, one that's common among firstborn children and among my family in particular. It's the role Mama's mother, Annie Raye, played, carrying the weight of her family on that dislocated hip every day for decades. It's a role Mama knew, too, stepping in for her own mother, straightening her brothers' ties as she sent them off to the dance. (One wonders if she ever went herself.) And it's a streak she might even have recognized in my father—the boy who dropped what he was doing every afternoon at 4:30 to make sure his mother was still alive.

The loss of Mama proved it to me: I come from a people who put their family above all else, for better and for worse. And with Mama gone, I'm stepping into the shoes she left me.

Jenna sent me an e-mail not long after Mama died, and it says a lot about the inner pain and defiance our mother lived with. "I remember thinking that her being on morphine in those last days allowed us to say anything we wanted to about her death and our love for her," my sister wrote. "It allowed us to cry next to her, because she couldn't have handled it otherwise. It allowed us to tell her what we needed to tell her before we let her go. She heard all of us, and you know, she finally did cry. Sela, it was perfect."

I'm glad for the window of honesty with Mama that the pain medication gave us. But it grieves me to realize how long she'd kept those curtains drawn. We were, of course, a close-knit family; I know Mama's whole life was invested in us kids. Yet there's a level on which I never knew my mother as well as I wish I did. I remember once, in my childhood, watching her talking and joking with Aunt Sarah's son, Tommy—and thinking, "Why can't she talk to us that way?" It may be that Mama just took her parental responsibility too deeply to heart, and never felt able to let her guard down with us. Or it may be that she just didn't know herself well enough to share herself.

As I've come to see all this about Mama, I think I've begun to understand more about my relationship with the land where I was raised. My friend Rina, who was raised in Israel after losing her mother in the Holocaust, gave me an insight into where some of my abiding love for Mississippi might have come from. "Like any child, I needed nurturing. But I didn't have a mother to give me that," she said. "I'm very attached to the land—not so much the people, but the land. I love how it looks, how it smells, how the earth feels. So I started to think of my country, Israel, as my mother. That saved me."

I know what she means. Everything I feel about the South contains echoes of the way I feel about my family: love, pride, protectiveness, that instinct to share and preserve and defend. I want my children to breathe in the Meridian I knew, while they're still young enough to have it imprinted on their minds. I want them to know what their own mama's world was like when she was their age, in every way—from its physical contours and pace of life, to the taste of the air, to the ways of the older generation.

Thirty years ago I moved away from Meridian, because things I needed to make me happy couldn't be found there. Now I come back, because so many of the things I need to make me happy can't be found anywhere else.

I'm not talking seriously about moving back full-time—not yet, anyway. I'm aware enough to know I still need the excitement and freedom Los Angeles has to offer me. I also love the transporting creative outlet of my work—something Daddy foresaw for me when Mama couldn't. But if I can find a way to bring the warmth and tradition and rootedness of Meridian back into my life permanently, I will. I'm as tenacious as Mama in some ways; I've spent the past ten years working on a solution to this dilemma. In so doing, I have made a collage of my life—a work in progress, its pieces ragged and

not always smoothly joined, but whose whole contains some kind of beauty.

And I'll admit that every so often I have to stop myself and stave off the temptation to think it'll be easy to reestablish a life in Meridian, to carve out a second hometown for my family. After all, the things I value when I go back home—the natural kindness and respect, the social graces, the web of close friendships among married couples and families—weren't bought and paid for. These things were built over many years of shared history and well-tended community. For a good long time, I may appear the prodigal daughter to some in this world. But I come bearing respect, and a good heart, and in places where I'm not known as family, I hope I'll be at least a welcome guest.

Anabella (right) with her cousins Anne Tyler (left) and Savannah.

When the train left Avalon, throwing kisses and waving at me
Says, come back daddy, stay right here with me . . .
Avalon's my hometown, always on my mind

—MISSISSIPPI JOHN HURT, "Avalon Blues"

*Howard and Austin
fishing on the farm.*

10 ⊚⟫

My southbound train journey is just about complete. I sit back and watch the desert scroll by through the window, and fall into a grateful sleep. When I wake up I can feel it's fifteen degrees warmer; the sight of Spanish moss greets my opened eyes, and I know we're in the South again. My sister, Jenna, will be there to collect me at the train station in New Orleans. And then I'll truly be headed home.

I think back to yesterday, about halfway through the ride. I'd walked down to the dining car for lunch. The seating for meals on these long-distance trains is communal; if there's a chair that's free, you take it. I'm naturally reserved, and it isn't easy for me to open up with strangers. Whenever I've gone to a new church, I have always awaited with dread the moment when you turn to the person next to you, shake hands, and say, "May peace be with you." I never have gotten used to sharing my solitude that way. But the day before, while boarding, I'd met a charming couple named Penny and Skip, who'd been married for twenty-five years; now here they were at a table for four, and I was glad to sit down with them for a quiet lunch.

A few minutes later, a fourth traveler came along to join us. She was a lovely woman, her hair long and splattered with gray, clipped back at the base of her neck and falling gracefully down below her shoulders. Her face was etched with beautiful lines; they made me wonder whether her life had been a hard one, or simply long.

Her name, she told us, was Jean. She said she was from Pontcha-toula, Louisiana, but as she talked I realized her accent was also laced with something else. When I asked, she told us she'd come from London many years before. Our food arrived, and Jean took a moment to bow her head and silently thank God for her meal.

Jean told us this was her first trip without her husband; she'd lost him a few months before, after forty-five years. Together we talked about how hard it is to suffer such a loss. And I remembered something my cousin Tom, the Episcopal minister, told me once: that everyone has a burden that seems just a little too much to bear.

Daddy is selling our childhood home. He doesn't want to live there anymore, and I guess I can't blame him. Jenna is taking it hard; whenever she's come back to Meridian to visit, she has always slept in her old room there, though she knows there's always space for her at the farm. I thought I would be just as sentimental about the old

house, but I find that I'm not. I take my consolation in the fact that we can give Daddy a place out here with us. He's designing a cabin he'll soon build on the farm; he's moved his drafting board into the Rose Cottage, where he's taken up residence until his new home is ready. After all these years, Daddy has finally stopped drinking and I'm so proud of him; he looks great these days, and to see his face now is to realize what an immense strain he was bearing during the last decade of Mama's life. Daddy's at ease now, and I'm grateful for it.

We work a bit at Daddy's that Saturday, boxing things up, and later on I stop by Hope Village to visit the kids. Then it's back to the farm. Jenna and her friend Indra have flown in from Florida, and my friend Martee has flown back down from Philadelphia. After a supper of steaks on the grill at the Rose Cottage, we all stretch out in the living room to listen to the frogs on the pond, and enjoy the restorative charm of a cool spring evening.

The loss of Mama is still fresh in our minds, and before long Jenna and I are talking about where we go from here. What happens to your idea of home, Jenna wonders out loud, when one of your parents dies? After relying on your mother or father throughout your life, how do you go about finding what you need within yourself?

"It's as though my own house has fallen down, and I'm having to build it back up, one brick at a time," I say. "And I know it'll be stronger, and the strength Mama gave me will help me rebuild. Still," I chuckle, "I wish I had an architect."

"Sela, you've been remodeling that house, so to speak, since you got married and had kids," Martee says. "You say your mama gave you the strength, and even if she didn't give you all the tools you need, your daddy's sure handing down a few good ones—confidence, brav-ery, that sense of self-worth. It's no wonder you want to reconnect with what you were blessed with here. That's where all your character comes from."

But there's something else I've been worried about, I tell them. My mama may not have had much truck with sentimentality, but I'm just the opposite—and I know it. Sometimes I look at Mississippi through lenses as rosy as our little one-room cottage. And I get car-ried away in the other direction, too: I'm just as prone to convincing myself everyone in Hollywood is soulless as I am to believing that small-town living is a universal cure.

"I know how warm my family and friends in Meridian make me feel," I say. "But Austin and Anabella are growing up, and making friends, and Howard and I are starting to make friends with their parents. And I don't know if it's just wishful thinking, but I keep hop-ing something more lasting will come of all that, too. After all, these kids' life stories are going to be blending together for years to come—on football weekends, class trips, prom dates. And most of the parents we've been spending time with actually seem able to leave their work behind at the office. Maybe I shouldn't be so hard on L.A. The days of me spending more time with my TV family and friends than the ones I have in real life are over. Life is too short to keep letting my career have free rein over my life."

Jenna goes into the kitchen to put some coffee on. "You know what I think, Sela?" she says. "I know what this connection with your hometown means to you, and I think you're right about it. But I also think what you're looking for is a way to find what you've been missing, and bring it into your life in L.A. If you keep reaching out and building those friendships, and putting the time in on the home front to build relationships within your own family—well, chances are, you can. I'm not sure it matters all that much where you're doing it. All those things you love about the South, those things that feed your soul—the kindness, the consideration, the intimacy of lifelong friendships—they're yours for the making. You didn't leave that behind when you left Mississippi. You can carry it all with you, wherever you go."

"It's like what they say," Martee chimes in. "If you want to have faith, start behaving as if you did, and you'll be surprised how easy it comes."

That night I lay awake in my bed, staring at the ceiling fan turning in the moonlight and thinking of this conversation in light of all I have learned in the wrenching year that has just passed. What have I been looking for, I wonder? The perfect blend of old and new, of childhood and adulthood, of home and away? Surely by now I must have realized how imperfect life is—a reality that has created fear in me. Fear I'm trying to escape—that old dread of failure, of disappointment, of not fitting in, and of being less than perfect. But fear is only an old and cunning trickster, and that's *all* it is.

It is time to realize that I may always feel a little out of place, no matter where I am. Maybe that's true for all of us, that fitting in is a fantasy, a wish that is sustained by the uncomfortable feeling of not fitting in. My longing for home—to be among the people and places I love—is real and true, but clicking your heels together and

saying "There's no place like home" only works in the movies. The Meridian I long to return to—and the idyllic childhood I remember—is impossible to fully recapture; indeed, it may never have been as perfect as I remember. Maybe the price we pay for moving on in life is this very nostalgic, bittersweet awareness of what we've left behind. What I've come to realize is that I must work to weave the past and the present into a secure fabric for my future—my own and my family's. First September 11 and then my mother's death illuminated a deeper knowledge that we are only given a brief moment in time to embrace the greatest challenge we face: to create an inner home for our true self.

I fell asleep as I always do when I'm far from home, thinking of Howard and my children. My life. My all.

A couple of days later, the rest of the Sherman clan arrived from the big city, and we all set out with my brother Berry's family and our kids for a trip down the murky Chunky River. The Chunky is the river of my youth; floating down along its waters in an inflatable raft is second nature to me, as exciting as a ski trip and as intensely pleasurable as a warm bath. I had a ball, the way I always do. Howard's still getting used to it, but Berry and his family love it as much as I do; his kids were in and out of the water the whole way, playing like fish.

My kids were hanging on for dear life.

Austin has always been a cautious child. He's thoughtful, tentative; he looks before he leaps. And he's as precociously analytical as his father. Even when he was just a few years old, and we were trying to get him to make the adjustment from using a baby swing to sitting up in a chair, he looked up at me and said matter-of-factly, "Mom, I could fall off and hurt myself."

But in the last year or two, I think he's finally coming into his own down here—making sense of the environment, internalizing the rhythms. He's starting to own the place a little more. That day on the Chunky we pulled off onto the shore for a picnic, into an incredibly beautiful little area. And there on the tree was a spectacle he'd never seen before: catalpa worms. They're funny little creatures, from the caterpillar family; cut in half and turned inside out, I'm told, they make perfect bait. (I wouldn't go near one myself, but down in the South ladies are still allowed to be a little squeamish.) Two years ago I don't think Austin would have had anything to do with a catalpa worm. But now he was fascinated, turning it over and over, letting it crawl up his hand. "Can I keep it?" he said, and I could not have been more thrilled.

When we got back in the boat to finish the run, Austin still looked a little wary of the water. He's a city kid, after all, and it's hard to blame him—the Chunky is one of our Mississippi-style muddy-water rivers, and there's no telling what kind of squishy things a pair of little feet might find on the floor. None of that seemed to bother his cousins, though, and finally I think their fearless adventures got the better of him. At last he made it out of the boat, and into that muddy water. And the look on his face— pride, and terror, and a little edge of giddiness—was all I needed to see.

Austin's just turning eight, and there's nothing I enjoy more than watching him. He's at that point where he's still very much a little boy, with a teddy bear and a bunch of stuffed animals still keeping him company—but he's starting to get a little too old for Mom to go kissing him in public the way she used to. Lately I think he's getting a little more comfortable in his own skin, too, throwing around a football, running around with his shirt off like his uncle Brock. His indoctrination into sports came back home in California, where school keeps him involved every season. But his real love of playing—that stay-out-all-day-for-the-sake-of-it excitement Uncle Joe talks about—is something I notice most down here.

With all that unscheduled time on the farm, too, Austin is discovering another talent: he's learning how to be a big brother. When he and Anabella were younger, he seemed a little taken aback by his sister's presence; every so often I'd see a look on his face that read very plainly, *A sister? What do you mean, a sister? Can't you send her back?* But in these last few visits he's been markedly kinder with her, patient and caring. They fill their days with terrific kid stuff—the blow-up pool, the trampoline, a Slip 'n Slide whose purpose he took great pains to explain to her. The other night, when they were jumping on the bed together, he slowed down for a moment and looked at me quizzically. "You know, I can't even remember when there was just only me," he said. "I wonder what that was like."

What keeps Anabella excited about Mississippi are her cousins Anne Tyler and Savannah. Back in L.A. we're usually too busy to spend a lot of time talking about Meridian, but not a week goes by without Anabella telling some story about her cousins. These days, though, I think she's starting to recognize that she's the youngest of the bunch, which is why I'm glad Austin is around to look after her. Like all the other women in her family, she's always had an independent streak; where her brother used to grow bored easily, she can lose herself for hours in imaginary games. But if there's one thing Anabella couldn't live without, it's Austin. She dotes on him unconditionally: when he comes home at night after a day out with the other boys, she's waiting by the door to wrap her arms around him and say, "That's my brother."

While we're down on the farm, then, the kids lead a different life, and the very thought of it makes me grin from ear to ear. They ride horses, tumble on the trampoline, pedal paddleboats around the pond, and go scooting about the farm on golf carts with their parents. And they behave differently, too. In the city they have a backyard, but they seem to need to be entertained all the time. Here there's no Nintendo—and they don't miss it.

Howard and I have a little game going these days. With the state of the world as it is, I tell him I've decided: I want to move back here for good. I don't really mean it—not entirely, anyway—and he knows it. He rolls his eyes and makes one of his gentle cracks about Southern ways, about the lazy days and the Waffle House cuisine. *You wouldn't last ten minutes down here, Sela.* But he doesn't really mean it, I tell myself—not entirely.

The other day he turned to me with a glint in his eye. "You

know, this afternoon I said to Austin, 'Your mama's thinking maybe we should move down here to Mississippi full-time.'" He chuckled, winding up for the punch line. "Honey, he looked at me like I'd lost my mind. Like I was *crazy*."

I gave him a good hard look, the kind I learned from Mama. "Howard," I whispered—there were other people around—"don't you mess with my Mississippi."

But then later that night, when he didn't know I was in earshot, I heard him talking to one of our friends after supper. He told the same story—"It was like I just told him the world was flat." But then he continued. "So, you know, tonight I asked Anabella the same thing. And she just lit up like a candle."

It is morning at Honeysuckle Farms, and I am standing by myself in the cool, dewy grass atop the hill behind the Rose Cottage. My mother is buried here. Someday we will all gather on this hilltop again, this time to bury Daddy. And then, years later, Berry, Jenna, Brock, and I will find our rest here, along with our husbands, wives, and children. This land, this good red earth, is ours, and we will be here forever.

My wish is that all of us should be gathered here together not just in death, but even more in life. I look out past the lakes and across the rolling fields, and think what a fine thing it will be if, a hundred years from now, little white houses have grown there like toadstools after the rain, and that in every one of them is a descendant of Annie Kate Boswell and Granberry Holland Ward. This is my gift to my family, even those I won't live to see.

Mama, I cannot give Austin and Anabella the childhood I had. But I can give them a home down South, where the people and the countryside can nurture them as it did me. I can give them grass to run barefoot in, and rowboats, and cane poles, and tomato vines, and horse rides, and lunches under the Picnic Tree. I can give them aunts and uncles and cousins, just over the ridge, to share with them the stories that make this place home. I can work harder to give them a home in Los Angeles, where they'll be raised to cherish above all else fairness, self-discipline, kindness to others, and devotion to family—the greatest legacy we Ward kids took from the childhood you and Daddy and our hometown gave us. I can also give them refuge here in Mississippi, in a place where somebody will always be there to take them in. And, I hope, I can give them the faith that will keep them coming back, the way their mother did years before, when they were young.

Mama, I hope that makes you as happy as it makes me.